ON WALNUT HILL

THE EVOLUTION OF A GARDEN

A.C. and Penney Hubbard's transformation of two acres in Maryland

Kathy Hudson   *foreword by* **Allen Bush**   *photography by* **Roger Foley**

**Published in the United States
by Hillside Press**

P.O. Box 482
Wilson, Wyoming 83014

First printing 2015

Photography

All photographs copyright © 2014
Roger Foley unless otherwise credited.

Photographs on p. 132 are courtesy
of Bonhams, London.

All garden history photographs courtesy
of A.C. and Penney Hubbard.

Aerial photo: © 2015 David Simpson

Design

Glenn Dellon, Dellon Design
dellondesign.com

ISBN

978-1-4951-6309-8

Library of Congress Control Number

2015909341

On Walnut Hill

onwalnuthill.com

Printed in the
United States of America

An aerial view of Walnut Hill.
Photo: David Simpson

ON WALNUT HILL

THE EVOLUTION OF A GARDEN

A.C. and Penney Hubbard's transformation of two acres in Maryland

Thanks Nick for all of you help!

Welcome to our garden in Baltimore

Hillside Press

Penney and A.C.

For Greg Otto and for Meg, Drummond, and Burgess Rice.
—*K.H.*

For A.C. and our family with love.
—*P.H.*

For Roger, Charlotte, Darcy, Molly, Kate, and Dónal.
—*R.F.*

This is the story of
the seasons and the years
in a garden and a family.

Allen Bush is the Director of
Special Projects for Jelitto Perennial Seeds
and Partner at "Garden Rant."

Foreword

One of Kurt Bluemel's signature grasses, *Miscanthus sinensis* 'Graziella,' blooms behind *Chrysanthemum* 'Hillside Sheffield Pink.'

The skies were darkening, and it was chilly. But that didn't matter. I was taking a walk through 40 years of warm memories. It was All Saints' Day, a good day to visit the Maryland garden of Penney and A.C. Hubbard. The tumbling pink daisies of *Chrysanthemum* 'Hillside Sheffield Pink' didn't mind the cold at all. There was lingering orange fall foliage on a witch hazel and yellow berries on an American holly cultivar. The bright yellow leaves of the Japanese maple, 'Sango Kaku,' were spectacular.

It would be too easy to say that the Hubbards' garden has been blessed. And yet I do think their garden *is* blessed. A blessing requires good fortune and devotion.

Good fortune arrived with Kurt Bluemel. The world-renowned garden designer, plantsman, and nurseryman, from Baldwin, Maryland, collaborated with the Hubbards on their garden for 40 years. Though known principally for introducing and growing ornamental grasses, Bluemel was an artist. There aren't many nurserymen with his good design sense.

Forty-one years ago, Bluemel must surely have been thrilled to meet Penney and A.C. Hubbard. Bluemel had emigrated from Switzerland a few years earlier and was just beginning his career in America.

Penney had a few square vegetable beds. Bluemel ignored these and said, "Let's begin with the perimeter. We'll start with the backdrop. The middle and front layers will follow." And he followed this with the advice that set the entrance to the house on an axis with pathways to accommodate two people side by side. The rest of the garden should be curvilinear, Bluemel recommended.

For the next 40 years, they listened to one another – the Hubbards and Bluemel.

"The swimming pool will go here," Bluemel said, driving a stake in the ground to mark the spot.

"No way, I've got conifers planted there," A.C. protested.

Bluemel always had a remedy to a roadblock. "We can dig them and move them to a temporary nursery and plant them back when we're ready."

Bluemel was a confident garden visionary. And he didn't mind taking control of the backhoe to ensure the job was done right. "For months the garden looked like a war zone," A.C. remembers, laughing fondly. Ultimately, Bluemel's pool design received national recognition.

The Hubbards are devoted to their garden. Devotion is hard work. A.C. dug *Taxus*, native azaleas, and rhododendrons from the old Towson Nurseries, in 1975, when it was going out of business. The "digging privileges" worked out well. Those plantings are all big now – and impressive. So are the Japanese umbrella pines and Atlas blue cedars. There are magnificent walls and small boulders, and the rock garden A.C. built with his five-year-old-son, Crawford, in 1975.

Trees, shrubs, and rocks form the broad strokes. Penney took care of the small strokes. Bluemel taught her a few lessons. "My variegated Solomon's seal wouldn't do anything when I'd plant five or six," she says. Kurt's recommendation: plant dozens. They were happier in a colony.

Snowdrops, daffodils, bluebells, and trilliums are happy in the late winter and early spring, too. Soon they are followed by impressive groupings of *Geranium macrorrhizum*, ending in the autumn with late accents of the yellow, fall-blooming *Kirengeshoma palmata*. Weeping clumps of *Hakonechloa macra* hold them all together. Never heard of the little-known, long-lived perennial or the Japanese forest grass? Bluemel's influence runs deep. The Hubbards understood clearly: you learn as you grow.

Bluemel was a plant collector, and the Hubbards fell under his spell. I hadn't seen *Ajania* (*Chrysanthemum*) *pacifica* – a Bluemel favorite – planted in years. How could anyone not be taken with this durable ground cover, which has tiny golden blooms and gray-green leaves? There is no shortage of the grasses and sedges that the nurseryman knew well. *Miscanthus*, *Pennisetum*, and *Carex* are here. He propagated and grew them, and could discriminately site them where they belonged. Bluemel and the Hubbards have a knack for this.

But Bluemel's fascination with plants wasn't restricted to perennials and grasses. The Hubbards like a rich garden tapestry, full of textures and colors. Weeping beeches, sweet-scented *Daphne*, and early spring flowering *Corylopsis* are here, too. Just as there will never be another Kurt Bluemel, there aren't many gardeners with the Hubbards' passionate curiosity.

I've visited gardens all over the world. It takes only a few minutes to tell when one is loved. (No doubt about that here!) What is special about Penney and A.C.'s garden is that it's so much more than a two-acre, hillside garden in suburban Baltimore. Wander the footpaths, and time slows down. On All Saints' Day, I wanted to linger. I was in no hurry. I was happy.

—Allen Bush, November 2014

Kurt Bluemel
April 6, 1933 – June 4, 2014

Photo courtesy of
Hannah Bluemel

> "No occupation is so delightful to me
> as the culture of the earth, and no
> culture comparable to that of the garden."
> —*Thomas Jefferson*

Introduction

This is the story of a garden. It is also the story of a family in their garden. The garden began in 1969, when A.C. and Penney Hubbard moved to Walnut Hill in Ruxton, Maryland, three miles north of the Baltimore City line.

The young couple had no inkling then that the garden they would create would become recognized as one of the finest in Maryland. They also had no idea that they would come to work with plantsman Kurt Bluemel, whose prominence increased during their decades together until he became the internationally renowned "king of grasses." His influence on the transformation of their garden turned it into a world-class Eden. Listed in the Smithsonian Archives of American Gardens, the Hubbard garden has been featured in national and regional magazines and as a destination for prestigious national and regional garden tours.

The acclaim and stature of the garden, however, is not what matters most to Penney, a retired public school teacher, private school admissions director, and community volunteer, or to A.C., a retired investment management executive. What matters most is that the garden has been at the center of their family's life, with A.C. and Penney doing all of the early planting and design themselves and, 46 years later, continuing to work in the garden and add plants to their collections.

From the beginning of their marriage to their present life with nine grandchildren, the backdrop of A.C.'s and Penney's life together has been the outdoors. Both athletic, they each spent much of their childhood outside. After moving to Baltimore in 1962, they discovered gardening. From the start, A.C. did all of the digging and construction while Penney learned everything she could about plants, trees, and design. In nearly a half-century at their Walnut Hill home, their passion and hard work have produced a masterpiece.

The Hubbard garden contains a fine and vast horticultural variety that is artistic and cohesive throughout the year. These two acres, restructured to create multiple terraces and filled with sculpture, are themselves living sculpture.

The garden has figured in all seasons of the Hubbards' lives: from the garden of young parents with three small children, to a recreational space for family activities, to an idyllic setting for a wedding, to a poolside gathering spot for grandchildren.

As Bluemel, responsible for most of the garden's final design, said: "The Hubbards have lived in their garden. ... This is a gardener's garden, a garden for all seasons."

All three Hubbard children, with spouses and three children each, now spend time in their own nearby gardens. All make a priority of spending time with their own family outdoors.

Seeds are sown early. Well-tended, and blessed by good fortune, they germinate, grow, and flourish.

Winter

Winter

The winter garden is quiet. After snowfall comes the deepest stillness of the year. A hushed white blanket amplifies space and armature.

Leafless, the garden form speaks. Curves interlock and embrace the house. Stone walls and geometric sculptures stand out below watchful trees. Boulders anchor the earth, their grip and mass more evident now that the plants rest below ground. Granite steps lead to the woodland, so dark and soundless it could be primordial forest.

If you listen closely, you can hear the weeping yews and conifers, the first inhabitants of this garden, whisper in a morning breeze. Light plays through needled textures. Glossy, satin, and crenelated blend. Barks are varied as skin. Greens darken to their deepest winter hues.

Nandina berries and scarlet 'Sango Kaku' shoots declare the life force of the garden, asleep below.

L. Azalea leaves create patterns on the snow.
R. Northeast view from woodland to expanded 1937 Colonial Revival house.

Acer palmatum 'Sango Kaku'
and *Hydrangea quercifolia* provide
winter color at the entrance.

L. Detail of Ilan Averbuch's 1992 stone *In the Cradle of Civilization.* **R.** *Cephalotaxus harringtonia* 'Prostrata,' *Chamaecyparis pisifera* 'Filifera Aurea,' *Rhododendron* 'Roseum Elegans,' *Sciadopitys verticillata*, and *Taxus × media.*

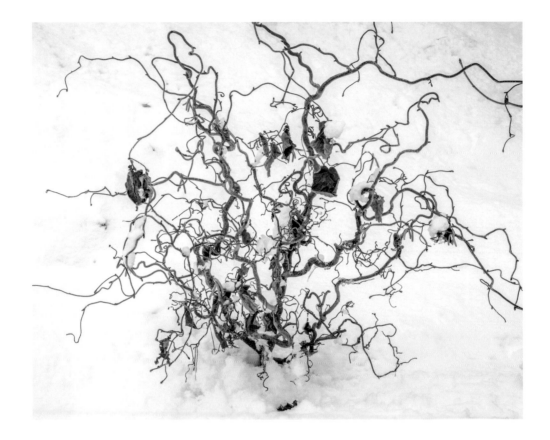

L. Kurt Bluemel's trademark granite boulders hold the hill, adding form and a sense of age to the garden. **R.** *Corylus avellana* 'Contorta' offers winter interest.

L. Untitled 1985 sculpture of six blue granite units by Ulrich Rückriem in inner courtyard. **R.** Asian sculpture on terrace wall.

Pinus parviflora.

L. A family antique American wrought-iron bench serves as a focal point of the entrance courtyards. **R.** *Acer griseum* adds color and texture.

L. One of a pair of *Fagus sylvatica* 'Pendula' that flanks the driveway entrance.
R. *Lagerstroemia* 'Natchez' and *Clethra alnifolia* with conifer backdrop, including the weeping *Tsuga canadensis* 'Pendula.'

L. Green Spring Valley vista with curved dry stone wall designed by Kurt Bluemel.
R. Evergreen azalea mosaic.

L. Antique pairs: Wrought-iron children's garden chairs; **R.** *Viburnum setigerum* overhangs English staddle stones that once raised barns off the ground.

L. Wreaths with locally grown *Ilex verticillata* on courtyard pillars. **R.** Texture: Relocated 1970s plantings, *Taxus × media*, beneath woodland deciduous trees.

1960s
SUNLIGHT, GARDENS, AND CHILDREN

In 1969, A.C. and Penney Hubbard moved with daughters Hadley and Kimberly (and son Crawford on the way) to a four-bedroom, brick Colonial Revival house on Walnut Hill in Ruxton, Maryland. Starting in the 17th century, the land had been farmland and later was an orchard. The Hubbards' house, designed by well-known Baltimore architect T. Worth Jamison and built in 1937, sat on a hill with almost two acres around it.

"I came up the road and knew that I loved it," says Penney. "The road was like a country lane. Big lilacs covered the front door. I loved the sunlight and that there were two acres. When I went out on the porch, the view absolutely captured me. I was able to look out over the ridges. I loved the sense of privacy, yet at the same time it felt open to the vistas and the sunsets."

When Penney told A.C. about the house, he said, "But we are in a four-bedroom, and we are going to move to a four-bedroom?" However, when he saw it, he liked it as much as Penney. They purchased the house in May, moved in August, and Crawford was born in December.

"Walnut Hill felt very rural in 1969," says Penney. "There was a chicken house in the woods and lots of horses on the hill. Best of all there was plenty of sunlight."

Sunlight had been at the top of Penney's list since she had begun considering a move from their shady hillside in town. Gardens and children, she felt, grow best in sunlight.

Both originally from Wilmington, Delaware, Albert Crawford Hubbard Jr. and Alice Penney Cox married in 1959. A.C., then 21, was in law school at Washington and Lee College (now University) in Lexington, Virginia. Penney, then 20, was a senior at nearby Mary Baldwin College in Staunton. Their first joint garden effort was tulip bulbs, which they planted under a window and along the sidewalk of their married-student housing in Lexington. A.C. dug the holes, and Penney planted the bulbs.

Those straight rows of red tulips broke ground on what would become a lifetime pursuit and passion. They were the first of more than 10,000 bulbs, trees, and plants that A.C. and Penney have put in the ground throughout more than 50 years of gardening.

While living in Lexington, Penney taught sixth grade and special education. Education was important to her Quaker-rooted family. When A.C. asked for her hand in marriage, the only request of her father, Hadley Cox, was that she obtain her college degree. She would be the first woman in her family to graduate from college.

In 1969, the Hubbards
moved to this 1937 Colonial
Revival house designed
by Baltimore architect
T. Worth Jamison.

"In search of my mother's garden,
  I found my own." —*Alice Walker*

L. Penney and Patsy Cox at play near their father's Victory Garden. **R.** Penney tending the Victory Garden. Her love of gardens started early.

After receiving his law degree in 1962, A.C. decided to pursue a career in business. He traveled with friends to New York City to interview at investment houses. Before he left on that trip, he received a call from Baltimore-based T. Rowe Price, a company he had not previously known. What was supposed to be a one-hour interview on his way from New York to the daily double at the Charles Town, West Virginia, racetrack turned into a lifetime career.

A.C. began as an equity research analyst, joining T. Rowe Price as the 25th employee. During a career of 42 years, he served in many leadership roles and as a member of the board of directors of a company that today employs 5,900 people in 14 countries. He also served for 17 years as president of the T. Rowe Price Foundation and played a key role in developing the foundation's mission to improve the quality of life in Baltimore.

When he and Penney moved to Baltimore, they lived, but did not garden, at shady 16 Merrymount Road in Roland Park, a planned, garden suburb established in 1891. The physical and architectural beauty of the community is still shaped by the original design and planning of the Olmsted brothers, son and stepson of the renowned landscape architect Frederick Law Olmsted, a firm believer in the beneficial effects of nature on human beings.

That principle also had been at the foundation of Penney's and A.C.'s childhoods. Penney lived with her family in Baton Rouge, Louisiana, during World War II. She and her sister spent hours outdoors in their mother's sunny rose garden and their father's rectangular Victory Garden planted with vegetables and corn. "Mother loved to arrange flowers," says Penney. "But I remember most the banana tree by the Victory Garden and the fragrance of the gardenia bushes around the house." Years later Penney insisted on gardenias in her bridal bouquet, even though the florist objected because they easily bruise.

Several times each year during childhood, Penney and her sister, Patsy, and later their brother, Hank, visited Longwood Gardens near Wilmington. "At the time we were not happy about spending Sunday with our stern, maternal Welsh grandfather, going to see stupid gardens," says Penney. "But we did have fun running around the tropical plants in the greenhouses. I think Longwood left a big impression."

A.C., whose early garden memories are also of Longwood, was an athlete and spent most of his childhood outdoors. "Basically, I grew up as a fairly physical person rather than a student," he says. "In high school and college summers, I worked in construction, at a pretty rough company, for 35 cents an hour, 10 to 12 hours a day. You had to be 16 years of age. My birthday was July 6, so I was illegal for the first few weeks."

A.C. played four varsity sports in high school at Governor Dumner Academy in South Byfield, Massachusetts. He was a Delaware state junior tennis champion and spent summers at his grandparents' home on Lake Winnipesaukee in New Hampshire. At Washington and Lee, he played varsity tennis. After college he took up squash and was a seven-time Maryland state division doubles champion. He became a national champion when he and James Zug won the 1991 U.S. National Senior Doubles Championship. He was inducted into the Maryland Squash Hall of Fame in 2014. His athleticism and love of physical activity translated well to hauling and digging plants with his wife and later their children.

Son Crawford's early memory of gardens echoes his mother's. "We would go to see my mom's parents in Wilmington, and I remember that on the Friday after Thanksgiving we'd end up at Longwood Gardens, not very exciting for my cousin and me. As a child you cannot comprehend how this could be considered fun."

Six years before he was born, however, gardening fun for his parents had begun. Their first real experience came in 1963, when they moved away from shady 16 Merrymount Road and rented a small, clapboard farmhouse farther north, in the historic, 19th-century "Rockland" community of Baltimore County. Their first child, daughter Hadley, was born there. At an edge of the open cornfields in their front yard, her parents tended a small cutting garden of annuals – zinnias, marigolds, nasturtiums – some grown from seed.

In 1966, they purchased their first house and returned to the city and the shady, Roland Park hillside of Merrymount Road. This three-story, brown-shingled house at number 27 overlooked the woods of the 40-acre St. Mary's Seminary, the first Roman Catholic seminary in the United States.

Their second daughter, Kimberly, was born here, as was the family's first horticultural investment. They ordered dozens of daffodil bulbs to plant along a low stone wall in the sun and for the shady areas, perennials: heucheras, hostas, and ferns. This purchase launched Penney's garden interest and her pursuit of plant information. The hillside terrain also began its imprint on the couple's gardening psyche.

Digging holes for bulbs and plants and taking care of the fallout from a massive canopy of old oaks and tulip poplars gave A.C. ample outdoor work on weekends. By then his career and accompanying responsibilities as an equity analyst were on the rise. Physical weekend work balanced the intensity of weekdays downtown. On Merrymount Road, the couple's pattern of working together in the garden on weekends from dawn to dusk began. "There may be no bigger satisfaction," says Penney, "than expending every last bit of physical and mental energy in the garden and coming in and being exhausted but happy."

L. In 1966, the Hubbards purchased their first house on a shady hillside in Baltimore. R. Family trips to Longwood Gardens: Penney's maternal grandparents, Willard Reese (left) and Ruth Penney Reese, with a family friend.

As Penney's family was about to expand, a friend told her about the house on Walnut Hill, on land that had once been filled with orchards. "I fell in love," Penney says. "It was a two-story house with French doors going to a long, open porch. It had four bedrooms and the original kitchen. The front door faced the property line instead of the street, which was curious for a Colonial-style brick house. The house sat on a mound that sloped steeply to a wooded area at the bottom of the property."

In the distance, in what easily might be the English countryside, was a backdrop of mature trees and the rolling hills of the Green Spring Valley. "Landscape architects James van Sweden and Wolfgang Oehme talk about 'borrowed scenery,'" says Penney. "Our borrowed scenery became that of distant rolling hills, tall trees, Hunt's [Memorial United Methodist] Church steeple in Ruxton, St. Paul's School across Falls Road, and, during winter, the handsome stone Marburg house on the hill above Seminary Avenue."

Best of all was the southern exposure with plenty of sun. For years Penney had craved a sunnier house and the planting opportunities bright light would bring. "The combination of sunlight and a blank canvas seemed to make anything possible," she says. "What began as a weekend hobby turned into a lifetime of passion and work."

When the family moved in, "the only 'garden' was a small, low, walled bed in front," Penney remembers. "One rock wall and a number of mature, deciduous trees – pin oaks, maples, locusts, tulip poplars, and a few apple trees."

Young daughters Hadley and Kimberly found new pleasures in country living. The neighbors up the hill had horses and a riding ring. "One morning A.C. and I were in bed, and the clock radio went on," says Penney. "The traffic report announced that horses were loose up on Joppa Road. We knew right away that those horses came from our neighbor!"

Penney Cox, age four, drives a lawn mower attached to her tricycle.

One neighbor kept chickens and let them run loose in their house. Meanwhile, the Hubbards' vacant chicken coop became a playhouse for the two girls, also thrilled to find a groundhog in the yard, voles digging tunnels, and owls hooting in the woods. Most exciting, and terrifying, were the colorful milk snakes and black snakes. "Weeding was always an option for extra allowance," remembers Crawford. What he does not remember is that his mother had to change the location of his weeding project three times in one day because of snakes. "She probably didn't tell me," he says. "Snakes were not a big hit."

Worms were. A favorite activity for him was digging up worms in the garden and seeing how many he could put down his father's back before being told firmly to "Stop!"

"And I didn't believe the girls when they told me a possum was in the window well," remembers Penney. "But sure enough, we had to put a slanted board down there to create a ramp, so it could walk back up."

In their shady Roland Park homes, they had had no grass. In the country they discovered the daytime smell of freshly cut grass and the evening scent of the loamy, moist earth and vegetation as temperatures dropped. "Honeysuckle was everywhere then, too," remembers Penney.

They found more bugs than they had had in town, especially spiders that scared the children. Webs spanned the front porch columns and the mailbox post. Lightning bugs brought nighttime games; praying mantises became garden helpmates, as did the dreaded bees and wasps. The slime and curling habit of slugs were discovered to be intriguing and "disgusting." Moles, frogs, and more snakes enjoyed the basement; bats occasionally flew into the second floor, and foxes enhanced the country feeling. "And so many birds," remembers Penney. "There were owls hooting at night, cardinals mating, red-tailed hawks soaring above, catbirds dive-bombing the family tabby

cat, blue herons flying in V-formation, geese in the fall flying in the same formation, pileated woodpeckers working loudly on the old shade trees."

In those days about one-third of the property was woods. A beloved Maryland arborist installed a zip line among the trees and a rope swing from a large elm. "My strongest memories are of playing in the woods on the swings and the zip line," says Kimberly. "We spent hours down there."

"And there were two crab apple trees I liked to climb," adds Hadley. "I would go up about 15 feet or so. I had a great view over the property."

The hill made a convenient place for sledding in winter, and for beginning skiing, when the toboggan was flipped over to create a ski jump. "The children would all be out in their snowsuits, which were pretty puffy affairs in those days, like the Pillsbury Doughboy," remembers Penney. "It was pretty sweet. The bickering stopped. They'd jump on the toboggan together, one on top of the other, for hours of cooperative play. It was somewhat of a contest to go farther and farther into the woods. They became so good at it, they'd end up down in the neighbors' woods."

Another country feature was the board fence covered in rambling roses that defined the northeast border of the property near the family entrance to the house. An early garden project was to clear out those contorted bushes. "It took two men in asbestos suits and blowtorches to do it," says A.C.

"It wasn't a job for the faint of heart or the Saturday afternoon handyman," Penney says. "The roses had been there for 30 years and probably never had had a haircut; they were completely tangled. Our first thought was that we would get in there and hack them down ourselves. It soon became apparent it was a serious takedown."

Early on, the lilac bushes by the front entrance also were removed. The family loved their fragrance, but they crowded the entrance. The area stayed blank until a Baltimore nursery planted azaleas and dogwoods. "In those days, you plunked symmetrical plantings on either side of the front door and surrounded it with azaleas," says Penney. "It was such a typical thing to do."

Also planted were English boxwoods flanking the front entrance, with another grouping under the front windows. "We learned two things from that experience," Penney says. "One was that the 17-year locusts were coming, and the other was that microclimates exist in gardens." Locusts especially enjoy new plantings, so each morning in early summer 1970, "I used my witch's broom, and I beat them off every inch of the newly planted dogwoods," Penney recalls.

After the locusts left, one side of the entrance plantings thrived while the plants north of the door, only 20 feet away, did not. "The cold north winds damaged them," says Penney.

A little to the west, on the bright northwest side of the house, came the family's first hands-on garden adventure, one reminiscent of Penney's father's World War II Victory Garden. "Victory Gardens were food gardens that reduced public pressure on the American food supply," she explains.

On Walnut Hill, Penney created a similar rectangle where three apple trees remained from the old orchard. "We planted zucchini, broccoli, tomatoes, spinach, and lettuce. Once, the kids cut into a first crop of broccoli and found worms. They were not too pleased. ... We also tried carrots, eggplant, and melons, and even corn, but learned that you need at least three or four long rows to have success," she says. "The plants were prolific and the zucchini big. That's when we started having stuffed zucchini boats for dinner." Hadley remembers sometimes using large zucchinis as baseball bats.

When it came to working in the garden, all three children remember it was never required. They were involved from time to time and weeded when they wanted additional allowance. "We never wanted the garden to be a burden," says Penney. "It was meant to be joyful. A.C. and I were doing it as a labor of love."

Yellow marigolds around the edge of a 10-foot by 24-foot vegetable garden were the first family experience with companion planting. They did not use pesticides, and marigolds help to control nematodes. To trap slugs Hadley remembers placing orange rinds turned upside down in the garden.

One fall, unripe tomatoes covered the vines, and an early, hard frost was forecast. "I picked up the phone and called my father," Penney says. "He said to pick the tomatoes and wrap each in newspaper. I followed his instructions and stored them in a cool, dry basement spot. We enjoyed fresh tomatoes well into winter."

Now with ample sunlight, and the planting and harvesting of a vegetable plot, gardening on Walnut Hill took root as a family affair.

Early view from porch toward
the Green Spring Valley.

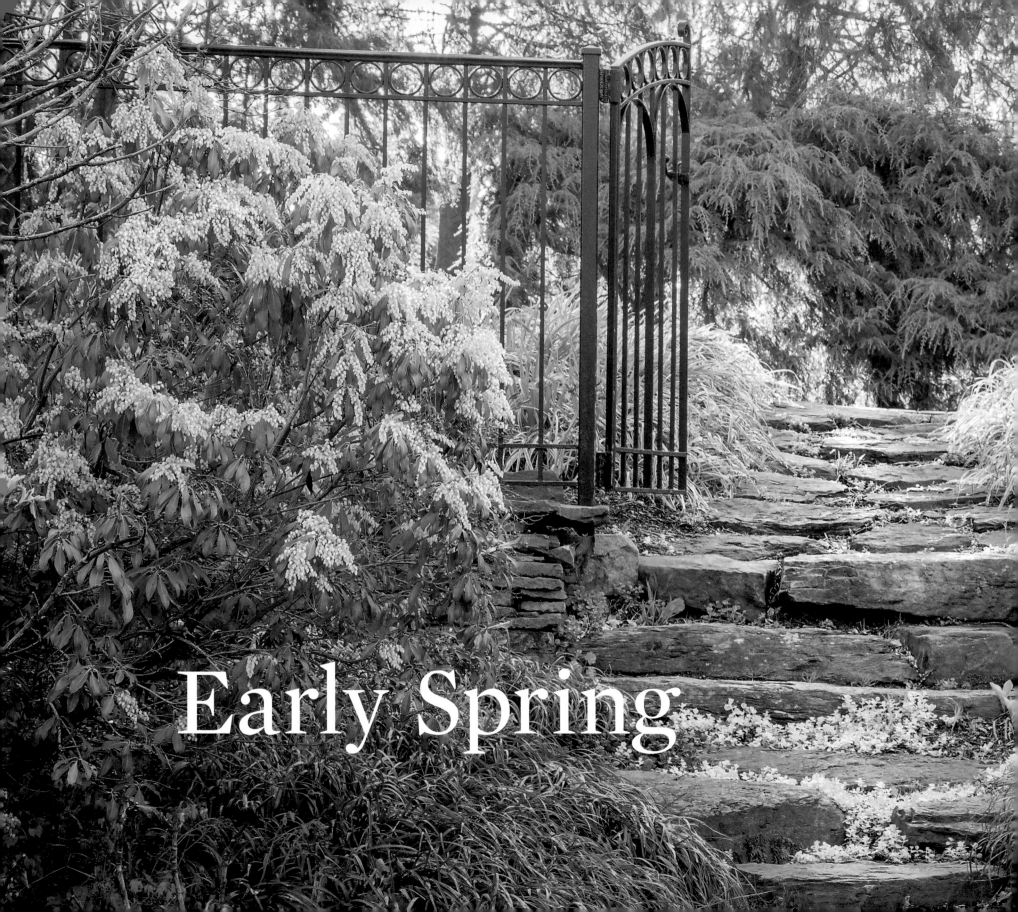

Early Spring

Early Spring

Spring is throwing a surprise party out in the garden. Confetti of celandine poppies signals the festivities are beginning.

First comes white: hellebores brightening the woods, creamy narcissus on the hill, leucojum in the courtyard. Andromeda and corylopsis festoon the garden in chains of delicate, tiny flowers. The garden lives.

Biting cold and brown leaves gone, the lawn greens. Florescence bubbles up. Leaves emerge on paths and trees, between the stones. The hamamelis offers spicy lemon fragrance. Threads and curls of new lime, moist like a baby's hand, say, "We're here!"

Ruby buds bejewel trees. Blue and pink pop open. Uncovered, the pool's warm water beckons. No waterfall yet. Anticipation builds excitement.

Trilliums' ephemeral faces appear, a miracle to see again, as are coiled fern fronds and scrolled hosta leaves pushing through the earth.

More color rises around the house, startling after winter's dullness. Yellow tulips, purple muscari, a paschal riot by the breakfast room. Daffodils gambol through the gardens, signals of color to come.

The gates are open. "Welcome home!" to the returning Hubbards. "Welcome home!" to the garden itself.

L. View from woodland garden with varieties of blooming daffodils and hellebores. **R.** Detail: *Helleborus* × *hybridus*.

Corylopsis spicata:
L. Fragrant pendulous bloom
and **R.** Against a textured,
evergreen backdrop.

Mixed evergreens, including
Chamaecyparis pisifera
'Filifera' and *Tsuga canadensis*
'Pendula,' by one of
two grandmother's paths.

L. Beloved woodland ephemeral, *Trillium luteum.*
R. *Scilla sibirica* 'Spring Beauty,' among 5,000 woodland bulbs enhanced here by yellow hues of *Eranthis hyemalis* and *Lysimachia nummularia* 'Aurea.'

L. Inner courtyard: *Acer palmatum* 'Tsuma Gaki,' *Pieris japonica*, and *Buxus*. **R.** *Larix decidua* 'Pendula,' *Tsuga canadensis* 'Hussi,' and yellow tulips above the lawn and Averbuch's *In the Cradle of Civilization*.

Ephemeral *Mertensia virginica* spreads throughout the woodland.

L. Woodland utility gate with *Mertensia virginica*, an English staddle stone, hellebores, and daffodils. **R.** Emerging hostas amid *Mertensia virginica* and *Stylophorum diphyllum*.

Second-floor views over lawn and relocated early conifer collection, including *Sciadopitys verticillata*, *Chamaecyparis pisifera* 'Filifera' and 'Filifera Aurea,' and majestic *Cedrus atlantica*.

Above the pool a wrought-iron
railing by Matthew Harris
with *Chamaecyparis obtusa*
'Nana Gracilis' on the right.

Pennsylvania stone used throughout the garden as steps **(L.)** in the rock garden and as dry stone walls **(R.)** on the upper terrace.

Chamaecyparis obtusa
'Nana Gracilis,' daffodils, and
a tuteur along path to pool.

Averbuch's sculpture *In the Cradle of Civilization* from woodland **(L.)** with the dormant *Davidia involucrata* and **(R.)** on the edge of the lawn.

L. *Helleborus × hybridus.*
R. Native *Cercis canadensis.*

L. Yellow themed woodland area includes *Stylophorum diphyllum* and daffodils.
R. Evergreen textures of *Osmanthus heterophyllus*, *Ilex crenata*, *Taxus* × *media*, and *Pieris japonica* 'Mountain Fire' create layers below woodland canopy.

L. *Cornus mas* sparkles with tiny yellow flowers. **R.** Teal paint enhances all garden greens, including a *Buxus* 'Green Gem' backdrop to an *Acer griseum*.

"When we try to pick out anything by itself, we find it hitched to everything else in the universe." —John Muir

Early 1970s

THE COLLECTIONS BEGIN

A.C. has been a lifelong collector. "It started with my love of baseball," he says. "The owner of the Philadelphia Phillies was from Wilmington. I started collecting the baseball cards that came with bubble gum and probably had 75 to 100 by the time I was 10."

As a student at Washington and Lee, A.C. ran the dorm concession stand and went through the coins before depositing them at the bank, thus starting his coin collection. In what is unimaginable today, the little Rockbridge National Bank in Lexington also let him count and wrap their coins in order to look for interesting ones. His collecting ratcheted up a few notches during law school to cars: a Model A Ford, a 1940 Ford convertible, and a 1948 Jaguar Mark IV drophead coupe he had shipped from England. "The best old car I had was the 1936 Ford Phaeton, a four-door convertible with roll-up, glass windows," he says.

Wine came next. "Our first 'wine cellar,'" says Penney, "was the top of a dry sink in our house at 27 Merrymount Road." A.C. says they did not start a serious collection then but enjoyed having a few bottles around for friends.

After the move to Walnut Hill Lane and A.C.'s frequent business travel to California, his serious wine collecting began. "When we moved to Walnut Hill, we found an old water storage tank in the basement that wasn't being used," he says. He built a trolley system, so he could push the cases into the large tank. When he wanted to use bottles, he climbed in and pulled them out. "Our first 'passive cellar' was that water storage tank, totally underground, with no artificial form of cooling."

A.C.'s first memorable bottles were a Napa Beaulieu Vineyard cabernet and a Chateau Montelena zinfandel. As his interest and knowledge expanded, French wines came next. Over the years, his collection has expanded to almost 5,000 bottles. "I put wine in the cellar for enjoyment with friends, not for investment purposes. Any bottle is available to enjoy with friends. ... I love the hunt," he adds. "And the quality of the objects we collect."

At age 78, A.C. still collects antiques, wine, and 18th-century English wine bottles and Black Forest whip holders carved in the shape of animals. His renowned collection of 18th-century English wine glasses, amassed over 25 years, was sold at Bonhams in London in 2011.

A 1974 family photograph shows A.C. and Penney Hubbard in the garden with children Hadley, Crawford, and Kimberly.

In the garden arena, A.C.'s collecting began soon after the move to Walnut Hill. During visits to his grandparents' summer home in New Hampshire, the family met a woman who propagated many varieties of hemerocallis (daylilies). "There was always a lot of hype about a trip to 'The Lily Lady,' and a lot of energy devoted to keeping the lilies alive for the trip home to Baltimore," son Crawford remembers.

At the end of each summer, dozens of different cultivars, diploids, and sturdier tetraploids were piled into the family cars: during the mid-'70s gas rationing, a Peugeot diesel wagon then later an Oldsmobile station wagon. The colors of the hemerocallis were always warm tones, ranging from yellows to purples, which were among the most unusual of the time. Early on, Penney established her garden palette of pastels in spring and warmer tones midsummer. "The purple daylilies were prized like the black tulip has been through the ages," she says.

Crawford also remembers ferns being dug in New Hampshire. "And I believe we tested the range of a white birch by bringing one to Baltimore, in a bucket in the back seat," he says.

On the trip home, the family usually stopped at White Flower Farm in Litchfield, Connecticut, for more plants. Hadley says: "I remember on the one hand not wanting to make our trip longer but also enjoying the stop, because the farm and its show gardens were quite picturesque. I also felt rather sophisticated knowing about White Flower Farm."

There they purchased as many plants as would fit into the car with three children and two dogs. "Sometimes the children would be completely surrounded by foliage," Penney says. Various pieces of driftwood collected from the lake would sometimes be strapped to the top of the car, along with occasional pieces of furniture from New Hampshire antique shops, completing the portrait of an American family summer road trip. On arrival in Baltimore, all plants were immediately unloaded to a shady spot for digging in during the following weekends. "We worked all day, and when it was too warm, we worked in bathing suits," she says.

A wide variety of perennials came to Walnut Hill like this, everything from columbine to coral bells, all destined for a catch-all cutting garden located beside the vegetable garden in full sun, 10 hours a day. "All gardens were squares or rectangles in those days," Penney says. "They were outgrowths of the Victory Garden." After the war, she explains, everyone came back home and wanted a plot of land. "The houses then were square, so the gardens were square. ... Like our house, our vegetable and cutting gardens were rectangular. First we cut a big rectangle for the cutting garden, but it wasn't big enough, so it grew bigger. Then we added another, smaller rectangle next to it."

The daylily and perennial collecting at the end of trips to New Hampshire continued for years, while the offspring of previous purchases increased by division throughout the garden. "With the daylilies, you could literally take a hatchet and chop them in half," says Penney. "It was not artistic."

Daylily division continued even after A.C. began his rock garden farther to the west at the same north end of the house. "The rocks were fairly small then, from the property, and could be moved without equipment," remembers Penney. They were gathered and deposited in the wheelbarrow. The spots for the rocks were dug out, the rocks carefully placed then packed in by dirt. "We wore out the wheels on our wheelbarrows," Penney says. "The rock garden, a new, less-square space, was our initial attempt at a 'designed' garden."

The design was governed by a slope where crushed stone was laid for a dry stream bed. The rock garden was also the beginning of 'curvaceous,' a shape considered to be a more sophisticated and visually pleasing form of design. A 1974 drawing provided a template for a dry stream bed, and an opportunity for A.C. and Crawford to do winter building.

Penney recalls watching the two work. "Crawford wore jeans, a striped T-shirt, his plaid down jacket, a heather green Shetland sweater or a sweatshirt. ... There wasn't much conversation. They'd work for a couple of hours, with Crawford either helping to dig or place rocks or using his toy trucks to move dirt."

Crawford remembers moving dirt as his favorite effort. "This was the point at which I realized the gardening was getting serious," he says. "I didn't totally understand the concept at the time, but I knew the gardens were going to continue to grow in that area."

L. Crawford, age three, helps his father plant upright yews and rhododendrons. **R.** Symmetrical plantings by the front door featured boxwoods, azaleas, and dogwoods.

Planted among the rocks was yet another collection, this time of conifers, inspired by family love of the outdoors as well as the mountains of New Hampshire and Virginia. Most were ordered from White Flower Farm, but some came from as far away as Washington state. In small cardboard boxes, delivered by the postman to the doorstep, arrived tiny seedlings of trees: *Tsuga canadensis* 'Cole's Prostrate' (a type of Canada hemlock), *Pinus strobus* 'Pendula' (Eastern white pine), and *Picea pungens* 'Procumbens' (prostrate blue Colorado spruce).

A.C. often gravitated to the ones that said "dwarf." Favorites included: *Pinus mugo* 'Mops' ('Mops' mugo pine) and *Picea pungens* 'R.H. Montgomery' and 'Glauca Globosa' (both dwarf Colorado spruce). "All were not dwarf, by any means," says Penney. "They would call something dwarf, and it would sprout wings in three years." The *Picea pungens* 'Fat Albert' (a blue Colorado spruce cultivar), for example, was labeled "dwarf," but now towers 20 feet above the garden.

L. The Hubbards' early conifer collection included a variety of *Chamaecyparis obtusa*, *Pinus*, dwarf *Picea pungens*, and *Tsuga canadensis*. **R.** Station wagon used for plant gathering by garage and house prior to renovations. (1970)

Neither Penney nor A.C. saw the heavy clay soil as an overwhelming obstacle. "We used a lot of gypsum to lighten the soil in the early days," she says. "Many loads came via station wagon when we were planting those conifers in the rock garden."

With the conifers, the Hubbards' interest in the garden officially extended to four seasons. "We began to notice how nice they looked all year, and the interesting shapes they took when covered with snow," says Penney. "I also started looking at books that talked about the garden in four seasons."

Top. Inherited wrought-iron benches created focal points for the entrance garden with a lawn flanked by *Buxus sempervirens* and a pair of *Picea glauca* 'Conica.'

Bottom. After the first renovation, the garage became a family room.

R. Walnut Hill children with Kimberly (far left) and Crawford Hubbard (right) by the rabbit hutch.

The next collection furthered the seasonal interest and came by accident: *Sciadopitys verticillata* (Japanese umbrella pines) brought down from Delaware by A.C.'s father, Crawford Hubbard. "When A.C.'s dad retired, he was working part time at a nursery in Wilmington, Delaware," Penney says. "There he met the head gardener for Mrs. Philip du Pont. The gardener had propagated a wonderful Japanese umbrella pine, and Crawford Sr. began giving us these young trees as presents for birthdays and anniversaries. At one time we had 17 of them, but several winters of heavy snow and brutal winds have decimated many." One stately specimen remains at the edge of the entrance to the woodland garden.

In 1974, a line of spruce trees on the northeast border replaced the white Colonial board and post fence, which had been there since the Hubbards' arrival. Hadley liked the pastoral look of the board fence and still remembers being a little sad when it came down.

Underneath the spruce, they planted a line of English boxwoods, plus two adjacent lines of boxwoods, for a total of 20. These additions created an evergreen border within the low dry stone walls that formed three sides of a rectangle and foreshadowed a rectangular courtyard to come. A pair of American Victorian wrought-iron benches from A.C.'s grandparents' home in Pittsburgh became anchors on either end.

Gardening was now a focal point of family life. "We happily trotted along collecting and planting higgledy-piggledy," says Penney, "building the rock garden, plunking down conifers, with lots of weeding in between. We were getting our feet wet, learning by trial and error."

> "I cultivate my garden,
>   and my garden cultivates me."
> *—Robert Brault*

Late 1970s
TRANSFORMATION

In 1974, A.C. and Penney decided, in spite of a small budget, to request a consultation with the rising star, European plantsman and designer Kurt Bluemel. Ten years before, he had founded a nursery in Baldwin, Maryland, and would later become known as "the king of ornamental grasses."

Bluemel joined fellow European plantsman Wolfgang Oehme as well as James van Sweden in introducing innovative landscape design concepts. Together they pioneered the replacement of rectilinear lawns and beds with sweeps of perennials and ornamental grasses.

Washington Post garden writer Adrian Higgins said in a 2014 obituary of Bluemel, "From his wholesale nursery near Baltimore, Mr. Bluemel was at the vanguard of a gardening movement … that championed the use of ornamental grasses and perennials as a way to bring nature, life and movement to residential landscapes he found achingly dull."

Penney recalls the first meeting with Bluemel: "It was an epiphany for us. We had been piddling around with small square plots and no overall plan, and we hadn't even thought about the perimeters." Bluemel changed all that. "Kurt took one of our garden hoses and began making lovely, sweeping outlines," she says. "We had never seen anything like this."

He also talked about the need for curvilinear edges and borders and a background for the garden. He wanted A.C. and Penney to think of the garden in layers: a tall, evergreen background with conifers and hollies; a middle ground with rhododendrons, viburnums, azaleas, and other shrubbery; and a foreground with perennials and annuals.

"It all seemed so simple," says Penney. "But we had never thought in those terms. So we spent our money on spruces and hemlocks and started our background. Is it Alexander Pope who says, 'All gardening is landscape painting'?"

Looking at the garden with this new perspective gave the Hubbards a sense of organization, as well as a new framework for their collecting, garden reading, and plant buying.

L. The Hubbards' 40-year collaboration with Kurt Bluemel began in 1974. Here, he is about to take a measurement.
R. Top. Original porch.
R. Middle. Original front door.
R. Bottom. Original north view with woodpile and shed on north side.

They began on the western side of the hill with the addition of dogwoods on the edge of the woods. On the north was a border of daylilies and a storage shed; on the east was *Picea pungens* (Colorado spruce); and at the south, hemlocks along the road. "This provided privacy for the family," says Penney, "especially when we had dinners on the porch."

Next, they started filling in the landscape. "And that made us start to think from the border *in* rather than from the house *out*," she says. "We never stopped looking out from the house, but we started thinking as well from the border in."

As the couple worked to fill in the border, opportunity struck in 1975. Towson Nurseries, on Paper Mill Road in Cockeysville, Maryland, was being sold for development. A fellow gardener and Ruxton neighbor, Floyd Lankford, told A.C. that for a small fee, he and five others could buy digging rights for any plants on certain plots of the nursery field. "We had assigned blocks," says Lankford. "And we had four seasons, two years, to dig. It was hard digging. We all bought special nursery spades with blades 15 inches long and 8 ½ inches wide and steel straps up the shank." Some of the plants were in solid clay. It often took two men to move one mature azalea out of the ground. Once, one of the men knocked himself out when his spade handle bounced back and hit him in the head.

Every weekend A.C., Floyd, and their gardening friends went off to dig, some with trucks and A.C. usually driving the family station wagon. "They'd leave around eight or nine in the morning, and sometimes they'd make more than one trip on a Saturday," Penney says. "To this day we enjoy beautiful weeping yews, native rhododendrons, and azaleas from that adventure." The weeping yews are now impossible to find at a nursery.

The first of many changes to the house came in 1976, when the garage was converted to a family room addition designed by Basil Acey of Gray Acey Architects, Inc. Dogwoods were planted, along with more boxwoods, to flank the new door. Across a new brick walkway, a low dry stone wall to mirror the original helped to create symmetry and delineate the new brick terrace. A modern, taupe wood bench on the terrace matched the new slatted, Texture 111 used for the addition. "Texture 111 was so '70s," says Penney. It also was used to create panels to separate the terrace from a new parking area built after Bluemel's recommendation to remove the driveway that went up to the front door. They followed his suggestion, and soon the driveway stopped just before the house began, at the family room addition.

By 1978, the rock garden and entrance gardens were maturing, as was the couple's pursuit of gardening. A.C. says that what kept them going was "the opportunity to be creative, to work outside in nature with an endless variety of plant material."

L. Family gardening: Here Hadley digs with her father. **R.** The first addition included a skylight and a unique chimney, with the 1970s siding, Texture 111.

Even the family dogs, Labrador retrievers and an occasional cockapoo, seemed to enjoy family time in the garden. "They were always hanging out with us in the garden," says Penney. "They would often settle down for a nap near where we were working, or when they were younger, they would romp around in circles hoping to divert our attention. Luckily, we never had a destructive dog. Not one of them was a digger! Maybe they knew that the garden was special to us."

Projects with A.C. and Crawford continued to change the property beyond the rock garden. In 1979, they dug an oval fishpond beside the new family room. With the help of professional masons, they built it with rocks to look natural. "This was a project right by the front entrance, a project for all who visited to see and discuss," says Penney. "There were lots of questions about what it was going to look like, how it would be watertight, would we line it with concrete or a liner, etc. ..."

The fish were never a problem. "The fish did fine even in the cold weather," says Penney. "They found a pocket of water under the ice and hibernated until spring. The plants weren't so durable. Every year we had to remove dead water plants and buy all new ones."

That year Bluemel also designed a new brick walkway to the front door, making it four feet wide. "Kurt taught us that you want a walkway wide enough for two people to walk and continue a conversation," Penney says.

In winter, Penney's garden focus did not stop. She took a "Design in Nature" course at the Maryland Institute College of Art. "And A.C. and I started reading garden books and looking at catalogs," Penney says. "We'd eagerly await the first catalogs to arrive in the mail in early January, stacks of them. We piled them up on the window ledge in the bedroom." Some favorites were Wayside Gardens, White Flower Farm, André Viette, Burpee. "We'd order from these catalogs, but, almost more importantly, we learned about various plants and their horticulture."

The combined momentum of collecting and learning about plants accelerated. By the end of the 1970s, the Hubbards' horticultural passion was transforming both the house and the land around it.

L. Crawford with the family Labrador retriever, Keji. **R.** Hadley and Kimberly with containers of geraniums and variegated *Vinca major*, a popular combination at the time.

R. Top. A.C. hosting a 1970s Thanksgiving dinner with a terrarium chandelier.
R. Bottom. Neighbors' horses often wandered Walnut Hill.

Late Spring

Late Spring

How could one six-inch-tall plant embody the profusion of mid-May?
And yet it does.

'Little Plum' lewisia steps out. Treasured gem of rock gardens, no commonplace bedding
plant, it sits poised in its warm stone trough, backed by soft boxwoods.

At first, it is tidy and demure, surrounded by fleshy green rosettes. Then suddenly,
its diminutive cancan skirts kick open. Phosphorescent salmon and pink blooms swirl
in a kaleidoscope of green.

As days pass, more 'Little Plum' emerges, delicate and stalwart. The bright sparks on the
entrance path shine as a hallmark of Walnut Hill.

L. *Hosta* 'Climax' with *Rhododendron* 'Delaware Valley White.' **R.** Shade-loving *Polygonatum odoratum* var. *pluriflorum* 'Variegatum' grows well in colonies.

Entrance path: **L.** Steppingstones flanked by *Pieris japonica* with *Epimedium × perralchicum* 'Frohnleiten' and *Styrax japonica*; **R.** Pale pink 'Nancy of Robin Hill' azalea, carpet of *Epimedium × perralchicum* 'Frohnleiten,' and emerging *Hydrangea quercifolia* 'Snow Queen.'

L. *Iberis sempervirens* 'Alexander's White,' *Matteuccia struthiopteris* 'The King,' and *Aquilegia* 'Winky Blue and White.' **R.** Kaleidoscope of greens: *Hakonechloa macra*, *Larix decidua* 'Pendula,' *Berberis thunbergii* 'Aurea Nana,' and blue *Amsonia illustris* at top.

L. Beneath the *Cedrus atlantica*, dark hews of *Acanthus spinosus*, *Aquilegia*, and *Acer palmatum* 'Red Dragon' punctuate lime *Hakonechloa macra* and *Berberis thunbergii* 'Aurea Nana.' **R.** Conifers, including *Picea pungens* Glauca group, surround Jon Isherwood's 1996 granite *Islander* with *Epimedium × perralchicum* 'Frohnleiten' underplanting.

L. A curved dry stone wall defines the lawn. Red blooms of native *Aesculus pavia* punctuate the green. **R.** *Acer campestre* and a native *Cercis canadensis* give vertical interest.

Matteucia struthiopteris,
Myosotis 'Victoria Blue,'
Kirengeshoma palmata, and
Acer palmatum 'Peaches and
Cream' surround a mature,
unnamed azalea.

L. *Quercus palustris* original to property.
R. Native *Halesia diptera*.

Cascading specimens of *Acer palmatum* resonate with the fountain wall.

Poolside views: **L.** Seating area; **M.** *Clematis* 'Madame Le Coultre;' and **R.** Northwest view from terrace shaded by *Acer tataricum* subsp. *ginnala*.

L. Lichen-covered steppingstone with *Aquilegia*, *Onoclea sensibilis*, and white *Cistus monspeliensis*. **R.** *Pinus densiflora* 'Umbraculifera,' *Larix decidua* 'Pendula,' and *Syringa* × *laciniata* and 'Miss Kim' as backdrop to *Spiraea japonica* 'Golden Princess,' Knock Out® roses, and native *Phlox subulata* on wall.

L. and **R.** *Gangakondacholapuram*, a 1990 granite sculpture by Wade Saunders, with arching *Acer palmatum* 'Seiryu,' mixed azaleas, and an edging of *Epimedium × perralchicum* 'Frohnleiten.'
M. *Syringa* 'Miss Kim' with rare *Acer palmatum* 'Butterfly.'

L. White bleeding heart mingles with *Hosta* 'Big Daddy.'
R. Contrasting woodland textures: *Osmunda regalis* and *Trachystemon orientalis*.

The entrance courtyard features white-blooming plants. **L.** Rhododendron 'Delaware Valley White' and Deutzia 'Nikko,' and **R.** on the other side of the wall, a weeping Malus × scheideckeri 'Red Jade.'

A 64-inch path creates
a wide central axis
for three courtyards.

1980s
NEW HORIZONS

Without realizing it, the Hubbards were becoming more sophisticated about garden design. With the rock garden they had pulled plantings away from the house and designed curvilinear borders, just as they had around the pond filled with waterlilies.

Making the well-established border around the property deeper and more curved increased the sense of privacy for both house and garden. It also provided an opportunity for more plants: dogwoods, hollies, and daylilies as well as viburnum and azalea bushes. "Repetition of plant materials creates continuity," says Penney.

The couple's commitment to a long-established weekend gardening routine provided time for new plantings. The routine enriched a busy family life, one that involved almost daily driving and attendance at the sports practices and events of three athletic children who ice-skated, skied, and played field hockey, tennis, lacrosse, and golf.

"We were always up by seven. We'd go out and garden, then drive wherever the kids needed to go and come back and work some more," says Penney. A.C. joined the board of directors of T. Rowe Price in 1980. "And he certainly skipped a lot of rounds of golf to be at home in the garden or doing a family thing on the weekends," Penney says.

L. In digging the hole for the fishpond, Crawford and A.C. had to remove a birch tree.
R. A.C. and Penney applied Bluemel's design principles of curved borders and an evergreen backdrop.

A.C. and his grandfather,
Crescens Hubbard,
in New Hampshire.

A.C. describes coming home to the garden after demanding weeks of leadership in a rapidly growing investment management company. "Working in the garden was a wonderful release, so peaceful and reflective. I would focus on the garden task at hand, and that would give me great satisfaction after a busy week."

In 1981, Penney went to work full time. She became the financial aid officer and director of admissions for the middle and upper schools at The Bryn Mawr School, an all-girls preparatory school in Baltimore where Hadley was a senior.

Penney worked because of a lifelong rhythm and personal expectation carried over from her student days. "I guess it was the Quaker thing, the strong emphasis on education. And what good is an education if you don't do something with it?" she asks. Penney can trace her impulse to work to her father and the summer she declared she would not return to the summer camp she had attended for three summers. "I was rambunctious. My mother described me as a 'handful.' My father said I was not going to sit around and do nothing, so I had two choices: to go to school or to get a job. Doing nothing was not an option."

Her first summer job as a sales clerk at Wanamaker's department store in Wilmington was painful. "I was so bored," she says. "I had to stand in the teen clothing department, and only one customer would come in. I didn't know what bored was until then. Bored is different from being idle, as when you wander outside or read a book. Bored was being stuck inside in the teen department. I went home and cried every night, but I had to stick it out for the whole summer."

The following summer Penney found a job teaching swimming to inner city children from the West End Neighborhood House in Wilmington. "It was much more stressful," she remembers. "Especially riding the bus with the kids to the pool way out in the country. That was crazy, but it was never boring." Being outdoors and sharing her love of swimming was exhilarating.

As an adult, working on the same schedule as her children fit well with family life. With the children growing up and Hadley about to graduate from Bryn Mawr in 1982, A.C. and Penney traveled more. They went to England that summer, and visited Hidcote Manor Garden, Sezincote House and Garden, and the Royal Botanic Gardens Kew.

"Hidcote was the first place I saw real garden rooms," says Penney. "The tall walls of hedges were dramatic. Going from room to room was like being in a maze. But seeing them didn't teach us to do garden rooms closed off by brick walls or stands of trees. It taught us that gardens have various areas, with more formal areas or less formal areas, areas of woods and areas of sun."

For example, an area might feature a swimming pool or a fountain. "Within the total garden you'd have various themes. ... And the idea that the entire property was part of the garden landscape changed our thinking to a total picture. The scale there is so much different, but it gave us a new way of looking at a piece of property." This, of course, prompted both Penney and A.C. to contemplate future changes to the garden and house.

More time for travel opened up in 1985, when Kimberly graduated from high school at Garrison Forest School, an all-girls preparatory school in Owings Mills, Maryland. A.C. joined the board of the T. Rowe Price Foundation. In addition to plants and wines, a new collection was on the horizon for A.C., one borne of travel.

Robert Bergman, director of the Walters Art Gallery (now the Walters Art Museum), knew of the couple's interest in Romanesque and Gothic cathedrals, so he recommended a trip to Salisbury, England. In 1986, Penney and A.C. went to Salisbury to the Cathedral Close and Mompesson House, where A.C. spotted a collection of 18th-century English drinking glasses.

He recalls with a thrill in his voice, "I had never seen such a glass. It was from the pinnacle of English decorative arts. What drew me to them was just seeing a totally new object."

Then in February 1987, at the Hunt Valley Antiques Show, just north of Baltimore, A.C. found a drinking glass like the ones he had seen in England and made his first purchase. "It was a double series twist with a dimple-molded bowl," he says.

"We were quite surprised when we saw it," says Penney. "We were used to going to antique shows, but the element of unexpected surprise when we saw that glass amplified it. ... It was an aha moment."

In May 1987, shortly before A.C. was made president of the board of the T. Rowe Price Foundation, the couple returned to England. They went to the Chelsea Flower Show for the first time, to Vita Sackville-West's Sissinghurst Castle Garden, and again to the Royal Botanic Gardens Kew. A.C. joined the Royal Horticultural Society, so they could have access to the flower show at less crowded times.

Penney's parents, Ruth and Hadley Cox, went with them. "They were very able-bodied," Penney says. "We'd go out in the morning and do a garden or some sightseeing. A.C. and I would go back to the hotel and take a nap, and my parents would climb on a double-decker bus and cruise around. When we went to the Chelsea Flower Show, we stopped by a grower of geraniums, and there was one called Mrs. H. Cox, my mother's name! Its blooms were salmon pink."

On that trip the Hubbards also visited Delomosne & Son Ltd., a well-respected antique glass dealer, then in the Kensington area of London. A.C. spent time talking to the owner, which furthered his excitement and understanding of 18th-century English drinking glasses. Penney fell in love with the glasses, too. The floral motifs, like the Jacobean rose and thistle, resonated with her deepening passion for all things horticultural.

Over the next 25 years, A.C. amassed one of the world's foremost collections of 18th-century English drinking glasses. By the time he sold them at Bonhams in London in 2011, with his family in attendance, the collection numbered 275. At the centerpiece was a 1766 The Prince William V, Beilby enameled and gilt royal armorial goblet that sold for approximately $186,000.

L. The Prince William V goblet, an important enameled and gilt royal armorial goblet, painted by William Beilby, c. 1766. **R.** A rare pair of Beilby enameled and gilt opaque-twist goblets and covers (c. 1765) includes fruiting vines, butterflies, and acorn finials. Courtesy of Bonhams, London

Top. Penney's parents, Hadley and Ruth Cox, with Dollie Sheffield (center) from Pennsylvania, at Chelsea Flower Show in London. **Bottom.** *Pelargonium* 'Mrs. H. Cox' discovered at the show.

mrs. h. cox

L. Crawford, Kimberly, and Hadley with their toboggan on the pre-terraced, sledding hill. **R.** Bluebird houses on posts beyond an early rectangular garden.

Influenced by their many trips to English gardens, the couple started naming various areas of their own garden as a way to pinpoint location when they were out working. They began to refer to the woodland or the terrace garden. Sometimes the names changed. "Because we'd renovate things," Penney explains, "we'd call something the 'new garden,' then we'd end up with an even newer area in the ever-changing garden."

Eventually, the intense responsibilities of work and raising children eased. In 1988, A.C. retired from T. Rowe Price, stepped down from its board of directors, and continued as president of the foundation. That year Penney also retired from Bryn Mawr. For two months the couple traveled in Australia and New Zealand. They then came home and thought about how and where they would live their new, more leisurely, life.

They considered moving farther north, out into the countryside of Baltimore County, where they would have more land. They were ready to put in a bid on a house. "But the house did not have a vista," says Penney. "And it was a house with a lot of road frontage on a road destined to become busier and busier. Suddenly, we thought, why would we want to be that far away from the city?"

Because they had always been intensely involved in the Baltimore community, the couple decided against moving. A.C. wanted to be closer to downtown and all that he did there – playing squash and attending foundation board meetings and other nonprofit board meetings at Bryn Mawr, Project Raise, and St. Ignatius Loyola Academy.

Although both felt they could leave the Walnut Hill house, neither was ready to leave the garden where the family had dedicated so much thought, imagination, and work. "The garden was very much a part of this decision to stay," says Penney. This decision ushered in a new era for the Walnut Hill house and garden.

Early Summer

Early Summer

June 2014 is greener than most, and the lushest in memory. The garden is a Rousseau-esque wonder.

In bright sunlight, hosta and mertensia leaves and fern fronds seem surreal. Wider, longer, rounder, the leaves keep emerging, more numerous than usual. Even blades of grass look chemically enhanced. Not so.

This verdure comes from long hours of charcoal skies. The rain starts. Garden lamps snap on at midday, as if night has fallen. Torrents pound the roof, the walkways, and courtyards. Waterfalls cascade over stone steps. Rivers sluice the woodland mulch paths. Rain drenches the beds. Nothing washes away: no flooded hillside, no rotting plants. Puddles collect only by the lawn's hilly edge.

Then the sun returns. Raindrops still *drip drip drip* from the house eaves, shade trees, even the heart-shaped epimedium leaves along the ground.

Droplets on the grass shimmer. Light gives rain its garden power. So does the rich earth, the sand, and loam. Deep layers hold fibrous new roots and old tap roots. They drink in the invisible elixir that creates the shades, sizes, and textures of emerald June.

L. Hand-hewn timber pergola with *Clematis terniflora*, espaliered *Photinia davidiana* on back wall, and ground covers *Vinca minor* and *Liriope spicata*. **R.** *Acer palmatum* 'Tsuma Gaki' and Rückriem's sculpture of six granite units.

Entrance garden: **L.** *Liriope muscari* 'Variegata' and *Hydrangea quercifolia* 'Snow Queen' in bloom; **R.** Beneath *Styrax japonica*, ferns and hostas (including tiny *Hosta* 'Lemon Lime'), and *Anemone × hybrida*.

Hostas: **L.** A collection at the woodland edge with understory tree, *Davidia involucrata*; **R.** Curves of hostas resonate with stone wall and blooming *Cornus kousa*.

Wrought-iron accents:
L. Antique bench with *Larix decidua* 'Pendula' and Knock Out® *Rosa* 'Radrazz;'
R. Matthew Harris railing with *Penstemon digitalis* and *Amsonia hubrichtii* behind.

Terrace tapestry of collections: Conifers, maples, roses, and perennials with *Kirengeshoma palmata* in right foreground.

After the rain: Arching limbs of *Acer tataricum* subsp. *ginnala* with varieties of perennial geraniums below and pink Drift® roses and *Cryptomeria japonica* 'Yoshino' beyond pool.

At the pool: **L.** A family gathering; **R.** The undulating waterfall wall reflects in the surface of the gray pool.

Woodland views: **L.** Original *Quercus palustris* on the lawn; **R.** A dense colony of *Matteuccia struthiopteris*.

Lime plantings add geometry and light. **L.** *Cornus sericea* 'Flaviramea.' **R.** (clockwise) *Lysimachia nummularia* 'Aurea' with dwarf hosta; *Hakonechloa macra*; and *Geranium* × *cantabrigiense* 'Biokovo' with *Tsuga canadensis* 'Cole's Prostrate.'

L. *Sciadopitys verticillata.*
R. *Clematis* 'Jackmanii'
trails on *Picea pungens* Glauca
group by Jon Isherwood's
1996 granite *Islander.*

L. Rain dances on north terrace by *Acer palmatum* 'Seiryu.'
R. *Clivia miniata* collection in garden room courtyard with Jon Isherwood's 1998 *Walnut Hill Fountain*; north terrace with Costas Varotsos's 1991 steel and glass *Horizon*; and Anthony Caro's *Table Piece Z-49*.

"The most noteworthy thing about gardeners is that they are always optimistic, always enterprising, and never satisfied. They always look forward to doing something better than they have ever done before." *—Vita Sackville-West*

Early 1990s
EXPANSION

Instead of moving, A.C. and Penney decided it would make more sense to add an office for A.C. Then the list expanded. "If we were going to do an office, why not do a wine cellar?" Penney recalls. And with the new office, they also decided to bump out the front entrance of the house to create a new front hall. This hall would make way for people coming on business to go directly to A.C.'s office. With an additional side door, it also created a new entrance to the garden and a new small terrace.

"We also talked about ways to bring the outside into the house," says Penney, not surprisingly for two with a preference for the outdoors. "We think it's important to be able to enjoy views from the living spaces." They envisioned opening up the walls of the house and adding windows and French doors for more light and garden views in the living and dining rooms.

While revising the first floor of the house, they decided to make some changes to the second. "I love to look at the garden from the upstairs windows. The bedroom view has always been an overview and a way to see form and shape rather than detail," Penney says. They decided that an old ironing room and a closet would become part of the expanded master bedroom.

"Then, I literally woke up one morning and saw the poppy wallpaper in the kitchen – large red and yellow poppies," says Penney, "and thought the kitchen has to go, too!" The kitchen cabinets and appliances were all in the very 1970s color, avocado green.

A.C. and Penney talked to their architect-neighbor Arthur Valk. In the fall of 1989, he presented plans for the addition of an office and wine cellar. These drawings created the template for sweeping redesigns of the house and the garden that would come about over the next decade.

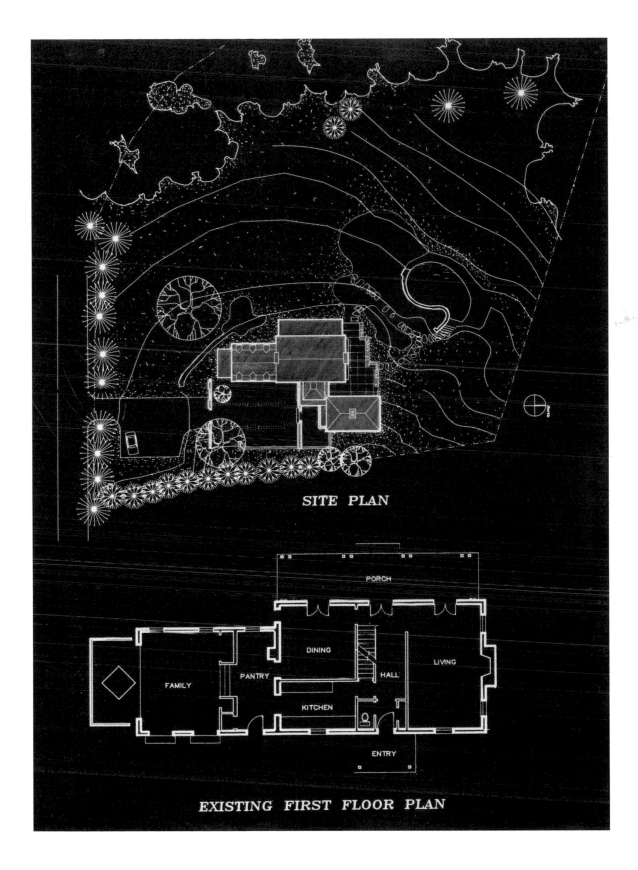

Blueprint of Hubbard property, including expanded house footprint. Courtesy of Arthur Valk

SITE PLAN

EXISTING FIRST FLOOR PLAN

PORCH

DINING

FAMILY

PANTRY

HALL

LIVING

KITCHEN

ENTRY

The first major garden
project included walls and
steps of Pennsylvania
stone to terrace the hillside.

The walkway to the new front entrance became more formal, changing the feeling from that of a Colonial house to a long European-looking house with a courtyard and staggered rooflines. The 1970s Texture 111 panels that had been used to screen the driveway came down. In their place, a pair of brick walls went up at the southern end of the walkway. These walls matched the brick of the house and enhanced the courtyard effect, complete with an antique Victorian wrought-iron gate that joined them.

The walkway, already 48 inches wide, was extended with matching bricks to 64 inches. This was even more comfortable for two walking side by side and made the entrance a bit more grand.

The walkway led to another pair of matching new brick walls and a small courtyard by the front door. An antique lead relief with a basket motif served as a focal point for a long axis that extended from the gates by the parking area to that new brick wall. "Creating this courtyard with an inner courtyard was very European," Penney says. "It made everything feel more intimate, too; there was now separation from the street and the place where we lived."

The new inner courtyard by the front door also provided a small gallery for the outdoor sculpture collection the couple had recently begun. The sculpture was always inserted into the landscape rather than having the garden designed around it.

By the fall of 1990, the idea for a swimming pool, which the couple had considered on and off for years, resurfaced. Again A.C. and Penney turned to Kurt Bluemel. "'It will go here!'" Penney recalls him declaring as he walked into the middle of the rock garden, up to his shoulders in conifers. "We were speechless. We just stood there and looked at each other, like it was impossible. But we are pretty optimistic people, and quickly it felt pretty exciting. It was hard to imagine at first, but Kurt was right." Bluemel's natural sense of artistry and his pursuit of painting made it easy for him to see where things would look and function best on a garden canvas.

He also suggested a diving rock (instead of a diving board) and the incorporation of tall rock retaining walls into the design of the pool to make it look more natural. An irregular design with a curved shape would, too. A stone wall went into the hillside, with a waterfall on the steepest side by the house. During construction, the mature conifer collection of almost three dozen trees was moved to a holding zone in a shady southern corner of the garden. A deep hole was dug, and the rocks were brought in. "It looked like a war zone!" A.C. recalls.

Penney remembers: "The masons erected a tent around that long pool wall, and they worked through the winter installing the stone fountain wall." The effect was that of a naturally occurring, freshwater pool and waterfall.

The waterfall wall offered privacy, more intimacy, and the feeling of being in an exotic retreat. "In the pool, you feel a million miles away," says Penney. Kimberly concurs: "When the waterfall is going, you feel as though you are in a faraway land. You certainly don't feel as though you are 20 minutes from downtown."

Now, because of the office and wine cellar addition, the pool was out of sight – downhill and away from the house. A new bluestone terrace for sitting and entertaining wrapped around the pool's shallow end, and a diving rock went into the deep end. In addition to keeping the water warm, dark coping and finish added another naturalistic touch. "A.C. and I wanted the pool to be well-integrated into the landscape," says Penney.

By spring of 1991, after the pool was finished, many conifers were reinstalled around it, and others were replanted elsewhere. Two new *Acer palmatum*, Hinoki cypresses, 'Nikko' deutzia, and grasses went into the pool gardens, as well as more hemerocallis, 'Blue Carpet' lobelia, pink echinacea, and blue camassia.

Boulders flanked the stone steps amid the new garden beds that softened the effect of so much masonry. A duck soon thought the pool was a pond and landed on it with her ducklings. "I called the Humane Society to rescue them," Penney says. "But a fox got them first."

All of these renovations took the house and the garden to a new level of design and stature. In October 1991, the renovations received Grand Award, Best in America Remodeling Awards, and an article in *Professional Builder and Remodeler* magazine.

In 1992, *The Baltimore Sun* featured the swimming pool, and when the annual national meeting of Garden Club of America was held in Baltimore in the spring, 24 delegates came for lunch and a tour of the garden. Maryland garden writer Dee Hardie wrote about the Hubbards' garden for the convention handbook.

In 1991, pool construction
included more stone for a
waterfall wall **(L.)** and
deep digging for a 10-foot-
deep diving area **(R.)**.

L. Raised beds, the original vegetable gardens, became cutting gardens for herbs, tulips, and dahlias. **R.** New steppingstones lead from a new terrace to the cutting gardens.

Horticulture was now 24/7 with Penney. From 1992 to 1994, she took George Washington University landscape design courses. They were held nearby, across the valley and beneath the green roofs of St. Paul's School for Girls that were visible from her garden on Walnut Hill. She studied plant identification, landscape graphics, botany for gardeners, and landscape design. "The plant identification course was organized by the seasons," she remembers. "We made five notebooks, two for spring." For each plant, she included the Latin name, the common name, horticulture information, a photograph, plus a pen and ink drawing adapted from horticultural expert Michael Dirr.

"Those courses for me were going back to my dreaded school days of having to memorize things," says Penney. "I recorded all of the plants on audio tape, with the common name, Latin name, and a description of the plant. I made three-by-five flashcards with the names. I'd climb in the bathtub and listen to the tapes. I spent hundreds of hours memorizing those botanical names."

In spring 1992, armed with a deeper horticultural understanding, Penney went to France with six gardening friends, who would ultimately travel together in varying numbers for seven trips to England and France. Internationally known English garden designer Rosemary Verey arranged and led some of them, giving her group not only insider tours but extensive design and plant information. Later that fall, Penney and her fellow travelers launched a series of talks and slide presentations to local garden and women's clubs.

That same year Crawford graduated from the University of Vermont. "I started thinking we might soon need a flat space for a wedding," says Penney. "I knew something was bound to happen." Kimberly was living in California but had a serious beau from Baltimore. Her older sister, Hadley, had already married Baltimorean Christopher Feiss at the Hubbards' Cape May beach house in 1989, just after Kimberly's graduation from the University of Vermont.

By February 1993, Bluemel had submitted plans for terracing the hillside that faced the northwest. According to Bluemel's plans, the hill, which had been used for sledding and skiing, would soon be turned into a series of curved terraces as counterpoint to the long expanse of the rectilinear house and courtyards above.

Just outside of the living room came a long and narrow brick porch, then a steep slope where Bluemel built three staircases of granite boulders. More boulders were installed in the slope to hold the soil and create more garden beds.

Construction on this major renovation began in summer 1993. Bluemel literally drove the bulldozer to site the boulders. "When Kurt started with the boulders, they did not necessarily end up in the exact spots as on the plans," says Penney. "But that is why everything looks like it's always been here, so organic and natural."

Below the rocky slope was a new curved, wide, and long lawn with resonating curved, low, dry stone walls at the north and south ends that subtly delineated the area.

Mature trees and some old conifers in new locations provided vertical interest to anchor the lawn. An existing pin oak stood at the south end, a sugar maple at the edge of the woods to the west, with both an umbrella pine and a blue Atlas cedar replanted near the center. Strategically placed, the trees provided balance and evergreen interest.

"All of a sudden we had a huge amount of sloped, sun-facing bedding," says Penney. After the conifers were resituated in the beds going down from the house, around the swimming pool and lawn, new plantings were installed. Among them: spring-flowering bulbs like 'Tête-à-Tête' daffodils and muscari; grasses; small shrubs like *Spiraea japonica* 'Little Princess,' 'Miss Kim' syringa, and polyantha roses; Asiatic lilies and hemerocallis; osteospermum (South African daisies); coreopsis; and corydalis.

The color palette was the one established by Penney decades before: pastels for spring and warmer tones in summer. Flaming red 'Lucifer' crocosmia and various shades of salmon to red salvia contrasted with yellow hemerocallis and 'Moonbeam' coreopsis in summer. In shady areas, five different varieties of epimedium formed the ground cover, and in sunny spots Penney used many varieties of sedum. "I also planted houttuynia, and we're still trying to get rid of it. ... Other plants I've lived to regret are mazus as a ground cover that comes up all over the place and *Lysimachia clethroides*. In the right place they can be wonderful, but beware."

With the terracing of the hill and the planting of more trees, shrubbery, and perennials, the gardens achieved yet another level of complexity and horticulture. While the design, hardscape, and plantings were well-integrated and cohesive, the pieces were many. Layers of plantings in more beds created a harmonious, unified, curvaceous, and dense tapestry around the house and down the hill. "And suddenly, we were into a high-maintenance situation!" exclaims Penney.

Finally, when they were in their 50s, the Hubbards brought in some help. First came Rich Gutberlet, who worked in the garden for two years. Ingrid Ernestl came next. Ernestl had gone to horticulture school in Germany, where she was raised, and had worked at the Holden Arboretum in Kirtland, Ohio, before coming to work at the wholesale Babikow Greenhouses north of Baltimore.

"She knew plants," Penney says. "And she had a disciplined approach to garden maintenance, and was thorough." When it came to box turtles in the garden, that was a different matter. "Ingrid was sure that one chased her while she was working in the garden." Ernestl worked two days per week from 1994 to 2010. Beginning in 2005, she often brought another woman, Teresa Smith, to help.

Ernestl's husband, Dejan, owned a landscaping company. He made varying sizes of containers similar to the antique stone troughs A.C. and Penney had found at the York Antique Show in Pennsylvania. These added low-maintenance plant variety to the formal courtyard entrance. He grouped them in patterns that remain today. "Even in our 50s we found trough gardening very satisfying and easy on aging bodies," says Penney.

By October 1, 1994, everything – front and back – was well-groomed and shipshape for a home reception following the wedding of Kimberly to Robert "Bo" Cashman. A white tent was erected on the lawn, with portions of the Corylopsis tree and *Kirengeshoma palmata* plants under it. White cushions were placed along the sitting wall on the east side for the party. The balustrade sculpture on the west side of the tent collected glasses and coats.

"We had been planning for the most gorgeous October day, but we had a major thunderstorm," remembers the bride. "Everyone came to my parents' house by shuttle from the Graul's [Market] parking lot. People came through the house, where we had the receiving line, walked down the big boulders to the tent on the flat part. I had to step down through the boulders in my dress. …

There was no going back after the skies opened up. We were a little cramped, but it didn't bother us for a second. It was actually kind of funny, except the wait staff had set up stations in the woods, and they were schlepping up the hill through the mud, having to roll up their pants. … But rain brings good luck." It also had rained in Cape May at Hadley's wedding, and it would rain in 2004 at Crawford's.

At the reception, flowered chintz tablecloths, ivy topiaries in a base of roses on the tables, and dark chocolate desserts fashioned in the shape of mice furthered the Walnut Hill ambience. "The next morning Mom had a brunch, and the weather was beautiful." A perfect ending to the largest family event ever held in the garden.

For her October 1994 wedding, Kimberly wore her mother's wedding gown. A rustic railing guided guests down stone steps to tents on the newly-created lawn below the house.

Midsummer

Midsummer

In midsummer stillness, garden layers reveal themselves.

Layers of green: avocado, viridian, forest, lime, teal, silvery, and chartreuse mingle, striated like the rocks around them.

Layers of texture: frilly and fuzzy, spiked and prostrate, crinkled and smooth.

Layers of shape: palmate, oval, oblong, hearts, threads, spatulas, and dimes.
Some defy definition. Geometry weaves the acres together, creating living sculpture around a rectangular house.

Amid the layers, midsummer's deeper blooming perennials – gold rudbeckia, magenta hibiscus, red roses – move the eye through beds and punctuate sheets of green.

On layers of decades, layers of rock and earth, midsummer evolves.

Focal points: **L.** Cool whites
of *Lagerstroemia* 'Natchez'
and *Clethra alnifolia* 'Sixteen
Candles;' **R.** Bright pink
Hibiscus 'Anne Arundel.'

Midsummer reds: **L.** Fruits of *Viburnum plicatum* f. *tomentosum*; **R.** Foliage and flowers of Knock Out® *Rosa* 'Radrazz' with *Hibiscus* 'Anne Arundel.'

Soft green texture: *Sciadopitys verticillata*, collections of liriope and variegated hosta near multi-stemmed *Davidia involucrata*.

Curved paths connect gardens,
adding a feeling of space;
grasses add drama.
L. *Miscanthus sinensis* 'Graziella.'
R. *Carex pensylvanica* in
foreground and *Miscanthus
sinensis* 'Morning Light.'

Beneath a *Styrax japonica*, variegated and blooming hostas add color, while *Hydrangea quercifolia* 'Snow Queen' blooms darken.

L. Below an *Acer palmatum* 'Seiryu,' *Amsonia hubrectii* begins to turn yellow and **(R.)** surrounds spent *Allium* 'Mount Everest.'

L. *Thalictrum rochebrunianum* adds delicate vertical interest. **R.** Backlighting brings out red veining of *Begonia grandis* subsp. *evansiana.*

> *"A garden should be natural-seeming, with wild sections, including a large area of bluebells." —Diane Wynne Jones*

Late 1990s
JUST ONE MORE

In the spring of 1995, Penney returned to England with her Baltimore gardening friends. They attended the Chelsea Flower Show gala preview and saw the Manor House at Upton Grey in Hampshire, with its Gertrude Jekyll garden that had been restored by John and Rosamond Wallinger.

Rosamond Wallinger's book on the process of the restorations inspired Penney to write about her experiences on Walnut Hill. *The Garden at Ashtree Cottage*, written by Wendy Lauderdale, the owner of a Wiltshire cottage that Penney visited on the same trip, also served as inspiration.

"I admire so much the perennial borders of England," Penney says. "It is amazingly difficult, however, to repeat those gardens in the mid-Atlantic because of the heat and humidity. Most people settle for a hybrid version."

Back at home, Penney's garden, in its new incarnation, required steady maintenance that was made all the more critical because of its regular visitors. In 1996, the American Horticultural Society came to the Hubbards' garden for a tour, as did the Horticultural Society of Maryland.

As the expanded gardens became a magnet for visitors, A.C. and Penney realized that the front parking area was too small. In 1997, an overall redesign expanded both the house and the driveway. Baltimore architect Warren Peterson expanded the south end of the house. To make room for four cars on each side of the driveway, Kurt Bluemel redesigned the parking area. By using the same Balcon pavers on the driveway and parking area, Bluemel transformed the space into an entrance courtyard, the third in a series of courtyards on one axis. A pair of stately, weeping beech trees flanked its entrance and hinted at the level of horticulture visitors would find inside. Other new plantings in the driveway courtyard included a yellowwood tree, an *Acer palmatum* 'Sango Kaku,' and a *Halesia tetraptera*.

Before beginning work on this renovation, Bluemel said to the Hubbards, "What are you going to do about Texture 111?" He was referring to the modern family room addition still surfaced with its very 1970s wood siding. "A friend was with me when Kurt said that," remembers Penney. "And her immediate response was, 'I think it should go.' So that was that, the end of the '70s look."

Top. Fellow garden travelers and Penney (far right) visit with renowned British garden designer Rosemary Verey, OBE, VMH. **Bottom.** Maturing trees by the Hubbard house with Texture 111 still in place.

In place of the former family room addition, a new brick addition extended south from the kitchen to include a new family room, a garden room for Penney's houseplants, and an office for her above it on the second floor. Just outside the garden room, the brick wall was extended from the Victorian gate parallel to the garden room wall to form a fourth small courtyard, this one offering an enclosed outdoor dining area. New York sculptor Jon Isherwood built a granite fountain on an inside wall as a focal point for the new family room, garden room, and enclosed patio.

Following this renovation, in the fall of 1997, Rosemary Verey, who had led Penney and friends on some of their private garden tours in England and France, came from England to Walnut Hill. "Of all our plants, she asked if she could have some of my *Carex elata* 'Bowles Golden' to take back to England," says Penney. "That's an *English* sedge discovered and named by the great plantsman E.A. Bowles, but it is finicky and dies out."

Following Verey's visit, Penney had an itch to do something more. "We had had the chicken house in the woods that had been used as a playhouse, and I had been influenced by the outbuildings in European gardens." First, Penney thought she would demolish it and replace it with a stone icehouse, similar to others on surrounding properties. "But I hated to take down the chicken house. It was such a country thing. Everyone in Ruxton had had a chicken house, so the chicken house was a little piece of history.

L. New driveway courtyard and a transplanted *Acer buergerianum*. **R.** Major equipment moved granite boulders and slabs to create the hillside gardens. Conifers were relocated, and thousands of new perennials added.

I also liked the idea that instead of having some formal thing [like a stone icehouse] we'd keep the shed-like look of a chicken house."

Again, the Hubbards contacted Bluemel, and in 1999 he submitted a proposal for the final stage of the garden to include a rehabbed chicken coop and the integration of the westernmost area of the property to the other gardens via a woodland garden. "This was a real collaboration with Kurt," Penney says. "Things like the rhododendrons and yews had been planted down there and were becoming pretty substantial. ... The woods seemed like an afterthought." Bluemel came up with a design for new paths to wind around the yews, the rhododendrons, and the chicken coop and then travel up the hill to the lawn and tie everything together.

The renovated chicken house was painted a stylish deep teal. It offered ample winter storage for all of the hoses, miscellaneous pieces of garden furniture, old dog crates, and the original French doors from the house. "Every now and again, I had a passing fantasy of having chickens," says Penney. "But I became cured when someone said to me that with two feet of snow you have to go outside and crack the icy water dish and add fresh water. That did it!"

In the woodland garden, Bluemel added extensive plantings: 5,000 bulbs, yellowberry hollies, a heptacodium, more yews, colonies of Solomon's seal and perennial begonias, collections of ferns, hellebores, rodgersia, and astilbe. Ground covers included

native pachysandra, arum, epimedium, and early flowering borage. All made for an orderly but naturalized feeling.

"The woodland garden is the crowning jewel," said Bluemel. "The entire plant collection is outstanding, with more than 120 different varieties of native plants in it alone."

Completed in spring 2000, the woodland garden added a new dimension. It captured the natural feeling of the woods and brought a diverse and refined level of horticulture to this last section, equal in stature to the rest of the garden. "As in the swimming pool area, you feel you are far away," says Penney. "If I go outside and just walk, that is the one path I always take. It's a great refuge. It also shows how in a small space you can create a place that transports."

Thirty years after the Hubbards moved to Walnut Hill, their gardens were complete. Both the house and the garden had attained such prominence that they were repeatedly featured in print and on tours. In 1998, they were the subject of an article in *Southern Living*. In 1999, The Garden Conservancy featured the Hubbard garden on its Open Days garden tour. *Baltimore* magazine featured "Penney's Project" in 2000. In 2001, the Perennial Plant Association included the garden as part of its Saturday Baltimore Design Tour. In 2003, the 90th anniversary of the Green Spring Valley Garden Club, a member of both the Garden Club of America and the Federated Garden Clubs of Maryland, was held in the Hubbards' garden. *Baltimore Style* magazine featured the garden in 2005, the same year that Ingrid Ernestl brought her protegé Teresa Smith, who continues to tend the garden today. A year later, the garden was part of the annual Ladew Topiary Gardens tour of fine Baltimore area gardens.

Despite the acclaim, the Hubbards were not ones to sit back and rest. Undoubtedly, inspiration would strike, and a new outdoor project would begin.

L. Hillside: Original view of excavation to create terraced gardens and, years later, visitors enjoying them.
R. Penney Hubbard and Kurt Bluemel discuss garden installations.

Late Summer

Late Summer

Wild is the late season. Plants roam, taller and freer in their September fling.

Slender Japanese anemones lean over the stone wall. They dance down the hillside, mix with troupes of Russian sage and roses. Cimicifuga and ligularia shoot up wands of white and yellow. Feathery plumes of miscanthus sweep across the windows. Pennisetum tufts sprout amid perennials.

Eight-foot dahlias, with globular heads of salmon, cream, and blush, fill the cutting garden. Beside them cleome bursts, lean spidery sisters.

Honey-scented autumn clematis sprawls over the pergola. Bees dart in to drink, as they do on 'Autumn Joy' sedum.

Bell-shaped blooms nod above kirengeshoma leaves. Across the path a slope of perennial begonias spills dangling pink beads. A peephole through the trees shows unexpected panicle hydrangeas; they look as fresh as their June oakleaf counterparts.

One by one, dried maple leaves fall, intimating summer's end.

Landscape lights: **L.** Uplighting
shows resonating shapes of
Acer tataricum subsp. *ginnala*
with towering *Quercus palustris*;
R. Backlighting of the hillside.

With blue-green accents of two *Picea pungens* Glauca group and an antique bench, *Clematis terniflora* on the pergola offers sweet fragrance and nectar.

Late season fling: *Perovskia atriplicifolia* and *Sedum* 'Autumn Joy,' with *Miscanthus sinensis* 'Graziella' and *Acer palmatum* 'Viridis' at top of hidden path.

L. September profusion of pink Drift® roses between annual *Melapodium divaricatum* and *Acer palmatum* turning gold. **R.** Patterns of nearby dry stone wall.

Cryptomeria japonica 'Yoshino' offers graceful, evergreen backdrop to a curved border of Drift® roses.

Anemone hupehensis
'Praecox' romps over
hillside steps and beds.

L. *Acer griseum, Acer palmatum* 'Butterfly,' and two cascading varieties. **R.** *Dahlia* 'Chilson's Pride,' one of many in the collection.

Sedum 'Autumn Joy' accents a Matthew Harris wrought-iron railing that resonates with the *Fagus sylvatica* 'Pendula' at the property entrance.

Sunset in the woodland highlights the varied bark of deciduous trees.

Landscape lighting brings romance to **(L.)** mature *Cedrus atlantica* and **(R.)** *Lagerstroemia* 'Natchez.'

"The love of gardening is a
seed once sown that never dies."
— *Gertrude Jekyll*

2000 Onward

A NEW ERA

The Hubbard family, like the garden on Walnut Hill, matured. In 1993, A.C. and Penney's first grandchild was born to daughter Hadley and Chris Feiss. By 1999, the young couple had three children. Meanwhile, daughter Kimberly and husband Bo Cashman were starting their family in California. In May 2004 at Ladew Topiary Gardens, Crawford married Ruxton neighbor Alexandra "Lexa" Baldwin. Today they also have three children, with the youngest born in 2014, giving A.C. and Penney a total of nine grandchildren.

All live within two miles, and three live right next door. Kimberly, Bo, and their two oldest children moved to a house on Walnut Hill in 2003. Their third child was born in 2005.

As soon as they bought the house, Penney started a new project for the northeast corner of her garden: the grandmother's path. "Once I knew they were coming, it went gangbusters," she remembers. While the flagstone steps and path by the corner of A.C.'s office were narrow and tucked away, fine plantings soon flanked them: a spruce tree, hollies, and grasses. "A couple of trees spilled over onto their property," says Penney. "When I told them, they said, 'Your spillover is our pleasure.'" Now the path is used all year, but most often in summer. "They can go straight to the pool from their house without feeling as if they are intruding," says Penney.

As for living next door to her parents, Kimberly says, "I see less of them than many people see their parents. ... But when they're in town, the kids love running down to see them."

Kimberly's childhood neighborhood now provides her three children with the outdoor experience and neighborhood friends she and her siblings enjoyed. With more extracurricular activities and heavy afternoon and weekend sports schedules, teenage life is different today. Walnut Hill still, however, offers the space to roam, easy friendships, and a country ambience.

And while Kimberly and Bo have quality plantings of viburnum, holly, *Cornus mas*, and yellowwood trees, as well as unusual tree peonies given to them by Kurt Bluemel, they are not the gardeners her parents are. "I'd like to have time to garden sometime," says the busy mother, who spends most of her time in the car.

After the grandmother's path was finished, fencing came next. To contain the Hubbard family dog Alonso, a Spinone Italiano, and to keep out the increasing number of deer, deer nets were put up around most of the two acres in 2009. "We already had the split-rail fence for the pool," says Penney. "We just backed it with six-foot-high deer netting on metal stakes. Behind each split-rail post, a thin metal pole went in." This proactive measure minimized damage from deer.

After Kimberly and her family moved next door, Penney installed a grandmother's path.

An enclosed sunroom for
year-round garden views
replaced the open porch.

The project for the following year was more extensive. In 2010, they decided to implement the plan Baltimore architect Vincent Greene had drawn to enclose the long porch overlooking the garden. "As much as we loved the concept of the porch," says Penney, "in Baltimore the combination of heat, bugs, and humidity made it so that we knew we would use it more if it were enclosed." Every year at Thanksgiving and Christmas, they had had a local tenting company enclose it to accommodate their expanding family.

As for opening the inside of the house to the outdoors, this final renovation brought a panoramic view of the gardens inside. An additional sunny room where Penney and A.C. could have their meals while looking outdoors was a bonus. For Thanksgiving and Christmas, they now set a table there for more than 20 family members.

"The sunsets at Thanksgiving are magnificent, with amazing layers of red," Penney says. "At Christmas we string tiny lights on the conifers. We look out on the weeping larch and the weeping hemlock that was given to me when I headed the search committee for a head of Bryn Mawr."

In winter, birds cluster on a nearby crape myrtle. Gone are its white summer blossoms. "But this plant gives back all year long," says Penney, "because of its spectacular bark, upside-down urn shape, and seed pods that hang around until spring when the first robin appears."

More garden changes came as a result of catastrophe. During the historic rains of September 2010, A.C. and Penney noticed moisture on the northeast wall in A.C.'s office, near the steps to the wine cellar.

The problem turned out to be a collapsing basement wall. "Water was moving the wall at about an inch or two an hour. A local contracting company shored it up during the storm, but it would have collapsed if nothing had been done," Penney says.

After the rain stopped, drainage experts and engineers spent several days coming up with a plan. "The whole northeast wall had to be excavated," says Penney. It turned out that when the addition had been built, the lower sections of cinderblock on this load-bearing wall had not been reinforced by concrete down to the base. Three or four feet of the wall were entirely without concrete reinforcement, so the basement was collapsing. Water was literally moving the wall.

In digging to discover this, the grandmother's path and its plantings had to be removed. All of the plants were dug out, with their root balls wrapped in burlap and moved away from the area.

At the same time, A.C. worked to find someone to remove all 5,000 bottles of wine. Miraculously, not one was broken in the move. The excavation of the cellar followed by the rebuilding of the walls turned out to be a three-month project.

When everything was finished and rebuilt, Roland Harvey of Natural Concerns, Inc. replanted and supplemented the landscape material. "At that time we added a *Cornus mas*," says Penney, who always finds an opportunity for a new plant, even in disaster.

While the Hubbards now contract with a company to provide house repairs and maintenance, they still handle a portion of the garden maintenance. When they are in town, A.C. sweeps, rakes, and prunes. Twice a week, Teresa Smith works in the outdoor gardens and on Penney's extensive indoor collection of clivias, ficus trees, orchids, sedums, Christmas cactuses, and, in homage to her mother, violets. Penney enjoys planting containers, new acquisitions, and deadheading. "I really enjoy pruning now," she says. "It is getting down to the essence. You're saving the essential and getting rid of the excess, kind of where I am in life."

As A.C. and Penney, now in their late 70s, have aged, they have considered the possibility of leaving Walnut Hill. "Again," says Penney, "I could easily leave the house, but I would have a very hard time leaving the garden. It is a lifetime of work and passion, so much a part of everything we have loved. It is our connection to the outdoors and nature. It's the surprise. I never tire of running outside to see what's going on: the bulbs, the trees. ... The seasons fit with the rhythm of life. The garden makes it very dramatic and very clear."

After briefly entertaining a move to a retirement community, the couple instead has thought of ways the house might again be remodeled, this time to accommodate them on the first floor.

Projects continue inside and out. In 2011, Crawford, a cabinetmaker, installed walnut paneling in A.C.'s office; the pool was resurfaced and tiled; and, by the stone steps to the pool, Maryland metalsmith Matthew Harris created a wrought-iron railing. The design of its graceful branches recalls the weeping beeches at the front entrance.

When some of the oldest conifers, the umbrella pines by the swimming pool, began to die in 2012, Roland Harvey removed them, and Penney again saw an opportunity for change. More lawn went in around the now sunnier pool area, and a new curved wall that matched the others on the lawn went up. Penney worried a grandchild might fall over it to a steep drop, so, instead of leaving the wall bare, she planted pale pink Drift® roses in front of it.

Teresa Smith has helped the Hubbards in the garden since 2005.

After returning from their summer home in Jackson Hole, Wyoming, in 2014, Penney decided that some other lively creatures, four-legged ones in the form of goats, might someday forage the "Bermuda triangle" in the far corner of the woodland garden. "When we did the deer fencing, we left out a triangular section of the property. Nothing is there but overgrowth and lots of poison ivy. ... When our neighbor was sick some years back, I had had it cleared and daffodils planted for him to see in spring, but now everything has been choked out by vines, maple volunteers, and ailanthus seedlings."

In Wyoming, Penney had spotted a golf course with goats in a pen. "I thought they were being used to cut the grass, and they were. ... Once we have the goats, and they do their job, I'll be able to get down there," she says with the keen focus that has driven all previous projects. "We'll get rid of tree seedlings we don't want and select what we do want then plant more bulbs." Penney does not see poison ivy as a problem or a challenge any more than she has seen many other garden conditions as problems.

Certain early plantings that she dug in with enthusiasm have turned out to be a challenge, because they were invasive: English ivy, houttuynia, vinca vine, and even Tradescantia.

The hill posed challenges in terms of its steepness and water collecting at the bottom. "The solution, of course, was terracing," says Penney. "Terracing is one of the oldest forms of farming and gardening and has been done for centuries all over the world. It's a great technique for handling a hill." Some would have seen as daunting the maintenance required on that developed hillside. "But I never saw maintenance as much of a challenge," says Penney, ever the lover of outdoor work.

The weather, of course, is a perennial challenge. Droughts stress plants, and hoses need to be dragged. "I never have had an irrigation system," Penney says. "I've always resisted because of the worry that it would drown everything if it went cuckoo while we were gone." In winter, snow breaks limbs, and the north wind sweeps around and zaps plants. Forty years ago, the cold wind killed a dogwood by the front door, and in 2014 it killed some Drift® roses by the pool.

A.C. and Penney Hubbard with their nine grandchildren. Photo: Rachel Lea Johnson for AmbiancePhotogroup.com

Never-ending plant acquisitions
include a recent *Edgeworthia
chrysantha* for year-round appeal.
Photo: Penney Hubbard

An optimist, Penney always sees challenge as opportunity. "The ultimate challenge has been the opportunity to learn as much as I can about the plants, the birds, the weather. ... And the biggest satisfaction has been experiencing the plants and the garden, then going back and learning why things happen as they do."

While away in Wyoming or in Florida for two winter months, she opens herself to new ideas for the Walnut Hill garden. Even with a mature garden brimming with plants, Penney pores over books and catalogs. "Gardening from the couch is a great way to spend the day, reading about plants and gardens and making lists for spring," she says.

With the onset of the Internet, Penney also enjoys reading garden blogs, such as "Garden Rant," "Red Dirt Ramblings," and "Everyday Gardener." For reliable plant information, she constantly refers to the Missouri Botanical Garden website. The one publication Penney never fails to read, wherever she is, is the newsletter of the Horticultural Society of Maryland. "It is the only publication that writes to our specific climate." Often she knows the plant discussed in the plant profile. "But sometimes I hit the jackpot and find out about a plant that is exciting to learn about and would be a great addition to the garden." A recent winter edition, for example, featured *Edgeworthia chrysantha* (Paperbush). Now one stands in a corner of the front courtyard just outside her kitchen window.

Crawford remarks on his mother's ever-increasing plant knowledge: "She retains it all! ... On a short hike in the Tetons a few years back, we followed a trail to a mountain lake, and up ahead I saw Mom hunched over, looking at the ground. When the rest of us arrived, she pointed out a small plant growing just off the side of the trail. It was only a few inches tall and quite beautiful. Many people had probably passed it by without notice. Not Mom. Very casually, she began telling us about what 'we' had found. It was a type of an orchid. I thought she was crazy, an orchid growing at 8,000 feet in the mountains of Wyoming. ... She told us all about it, including its Latin name [*Calypso bulbosa*], and it became clear that we were looking at something pretty special."

He particularly appreciates that his mother's vast plant knowledge is all rooted in curiosity. "Mom will always pass along tidbits when asked and does so with an inflection that would have you believe she is new to the information herself. ... She makes it feel as if you are part of the journey."

"And one thing is constant about the journey," Penney says. "Gardens are ever-changing. Through storms, wind, rain, and snow, gardens will suffer, but they will come back. They will be different, but they will come back. If you decide to garden, know that gardens are ever-changing."

Autumn

Autumn

Days before the first frost, golden light bathes a radiant garden at ease. This is the majestic last hurrah.

Leaves strew the paths, adorn the beds, and float on cooling water. Brown, red, and gold mosaics overlay the most vibrant green since spring. Liriope flops beside a path. Almost-spent Japanese anemones careen helter-skelter. Their cottony seed heads pop open with tufts.

Cars drone louder across the more barren valley. Cricket chirps weaken.

New smells permeate the grounds: the smoky scent of drying leaves, a pungent bite of haywire Russian sage.

Final blooms, precious and iridescent, appear on the rose bushes, the asters, the dahlias. The end of season shows such joy.

Spreading colors radiate. Gold on feathery *Amsonia hubrectii*, gold plates of hostas, golden tulip poplars about to set loose their autumnal cascade. What triggers a tree to let go?

Crimson fills the disanthus and rises in old acers, as brilliant now as plump new viburnum berries, next season's life. A final blood-red surge will soon enflame the garden.

L. By the plant room, *Acer palmatum* 'Koto No Ito' in front of gold *Acer palmatum* 'Sango Kaku.'
R. *Ilex verticillata*, *Perovskia atriplicifolia*, and *Dryopteris erythrosora* 'Brilliance.'

L. *Quercus palustris*, red-leaved *Cornus florida*, yellow *Corylopsis spicata*, and *Cercis canadensis*. **M.** *Quercus palustris* and *Acer palmatum* 'Sango Kaku.' **R.** *Hydrangea paniculata* 'Tardiva' and *Picea abies*.

Leaves of *Acer palmatum* 'Viridis' hold color for weeks before dropping.

Evergreen *Chamaecyparis obtusa* 'Nana Gracilis' enhances fall color of *Acer palmatum* 'Viridis' (left), *Acer palmatum* 'Seiryu' (above), and *Disanthus cercidifolius*.

Gold: **L.** Towering *Acer saccharum*; **R.** *Acer palmatum* 'Sango Kaku.'

Turning yellow: *Styrax japonica,*
Hosta, Matteuccia struthiopteris
with *Corylopsis spicata* on
leaf-covered lawn.

Fall hillside: White *Nipponanthemum nipponicum*, *Hakonechloa macra*, bronze *Spiraea japonica* 'Golden Princess,' lavender *Perovskia atriplicifolia*, and red Knock Out® *Rosa* 'Radrazz.'

L. Delicate *Acer palmatum* 'Butterfly' and *Amsonia hubrechtii.*
R. *Amsonia hubrechtii* with *Sedum* 'Autumn Joy.'

Leaf mosaics: **L.** *Styrax
japonica, Cornus florida,
Corylopsis spicata,* and
Kirengeshoma palmata;
R. *Corylopsis spicata* detail.

L. Late blooms of *Hydrangea paniculata* 'Tardiva' with turning *Cornus kousa*. **R.** *Hosta* 'Royal Standard' and *Cornus kousa*.

L. Antique stone penguins
below contorted branches of
Acer palmatum. **R.** *Hydrangea
quercifolia* 'Snow Queen.'

"Tree at my window, window tree,
My sash is lowered when night comes on;
But let there never be curtain drawn
Between you and me."

From "Tree at My Window" by Robert Frost

> *"How beautifully leaves grow old.
> How full of light and color are their
> last days." —John Burroughs*

Reflections

Penney pauses in the woodland garden, with the flaming tree canopy above her. "Fall has come as one of the biggest surprises," she says. "It is more than beautiful leaves and putting on a wool skirt and going to a football game. Fall is one of the most spectacular times in the garden: the pods, the seeds, the color. We get so much growth in the fall here, a resurgence, after the heat and humidity that seem to stall things during Baltimore summers."

For Penney, who has always preferred a natural look in her garden – tidy, but not formal or overly manicured – the relaxed look of the fall garden comes as a special reward at the end of the growing season.

Before the first frost, a final burst of roses offers blooms and new height. Colors of annuals become florescent. Grasses waft across the hill. A stand of *Amsonia hubrechtii* by the pool turns feathery gold. Arcs of yellow Solomon's seal shine by sweeps of still-green ferns. Pods on perennial begonia dangle in the woodland garden. Leaves fall into a rich mosaic around everything.

"Things that are still green and had turned slightly dull or brown have a resurgence of vibrant green again," says Penney. "That green contrasts with the changing color, making it all the more dramatic."

In their early days on Walnut Hill, A.C. and Penney might have been too busy planting conifers and bulbs, raking, or pondering the next project to sit back and take in full fall splendor. While forward momentum, in the garden and life, still engages them, they now find more time to stroll or sit and enjoy the views across the valley and over the terraces.

Penney believes that the fact that their garden is on two acres and not 200, like a Rockefeller garden, makes it "grabbable." She thinks anyone with dedication can create a beautiful garden. "We have been fortunate in recent years to have resources, but we did much of it in the early days ourselves. Youth and ignorance can be an asset. You just forge ahead and ask later. You don't realize there's a challenge until the obstacles meet you. Later you ask, 'What were we thinking?'" She adds, "We weren't thinking. We were just going for something that was exciting. We had no idea how it was going to be executed, but we had the full energy and confidence of youth, blind exuberance."

Daylilies were one of the
Hubbards' first plant
collections. This burgundy
variety came from
New Hampshire.
Photo: Penney Hubbard

No matter where they are, Penney and A.C. spend time outdoors, together and separately, tending their garden. The ingrained rhythm of gardening has become the rhythm of their life, constant during a half-century together.

The continuity in their Walnut Hill garden adds particular meaning. First there are the trees and plants grown from the earliest days. Then there are the people. Both the son and grandson of the couple responsible for introducing them to Baltimore, and later to Walnut Hill, work regularly on the property. For more than 10 years, Teresa Smith has tended the garden. Alexander Betz, the grandson of the late Kurt Bluemel, whose artistry still governs the garden, visits and emails with plant advice. Penney and Bluemel's widow, Hannah, are in touch.

"Kurt was a good choice for us," Penney reflects. "He was a true plantsman and did not mind my being excited by a plant and plunking it down in a spot that might interrupt his 'sweep.'" Undoubtedly, he would have been proud that their garden was featured again on a tour by the Perennial Plant Association, this time during its 33rd Perennial Plant Symposium in July 2015.

The Hubbards derive immeasurable satisfaction from having children and grandchildren so close. Penney and A.C. offer the next generations the rich intangibles of a large, in-town, multi-generational family, something their children did not have growing up. Hadley, whose children are the oldest, says that her children have spent a lot of time with their cousins on the weekends, holidays, and at a camp in Maine. "It was like having part-time siblings. ... Now they make special plans for biking together or playing squash. Thanksgiving Day, everyone gets together for a parent-child soccer match that includes many family friends from the area."

Crawford, an outdoor enthusiast and cabinetmaker, returned to Baltimore from California even before he married Lexa. Their three children are the youngest of the grandchildren and cousins. "They were all born in town and have known their grandparents on both sides their entire lives," he says. "Every Wednesday Mom takes our oldest to school and picks her up."

Being in the same town with their families is why Kimberly and her husband, Bo, moved back from the West Coast more than a decade ago. "We hope that those family connections will always keep our kids grounded as they grow up and go away from home," Kimberly says.

And as for the grandmother: "Our children are now our best friends," says Penney. "When we are in town, we spend time together and consult each other on everything. If a phone call starts, 'I need a consultation,' that means to stop over and help with a paint color, a plant that needs placing, a purchase decision, a health concern, or a down moment. We talk about child-rearing, community involvement, financial investing, the best new restaurant, good books. We have spur-of-the-moment crab feasts, Sunday suppers, and leftover nights. And we have plenty of laughs over a mystery bottle of wine."

"It has been a great blessing for me to have so greatly enjoyed so much, both my professional life here and the other activities including gardening, collecting, playing squash, and the family," adds A.C.

The grandchildren are the icing on the cake. "It is pure joy to have them close for family celebrations and holidays," says Penney. "But in some ways it's the other, daily things that make it so special – the young granddaughter who knows you well enough to call you 'chicken head,' a grandson dressed on Halloween as a piece of cheese, a pair of socks left behind by one, watching them play lots of sports, attending a grandson's rock concert, going shopping or playing the piano with granddaughters, getting to know one's boyfriend, doing puzzles and endless games of Old Maid."

As they grow older, A.C. and Penney also find comfort in having the younger generations close. "I was puzzled when a friend decided to move to another state to a retirement community to be near her son and his family," Penney remembers. "Now I get it," she says, bending down to examine the re-blooming of a Robin Hill azalea on a fall day.

Even when its leaves are brown from frost, an azalea or a rose sometimes blooms. "The trigger of the bloom is light," she explains. "There is a certain time in spring and fall when the length of the day is the same, and the plant gets tricked into blooming."

One can easily imagine a vibrant gardener and an ardent collector, one day in their 90s, in just the same way: surrounded by mature, well-tended trees and fully planted gardens with a bright new project, blooming.

A.C. and Penney Hubbard
in their spring garden.
Photo: Chris Hartlove

Resources

A & A Tree Experts, Inc.
7081 Milford Industrial Road
Pikesville, Maryland 21208
410 486 4561
aatreeexperts.com

The Behnke Nurseries Co.
11300 Baltimore Avenue
Beltsville, Maryland 20705
301 937 1100
behnkes.com

Kurt Bluemel, Inc.
2740 Greene Lane
Baldwin, Maryland 21013
800 498 1560
kurtbluemel.com

Brent and Becky's Bulbs
7900 Daffodil Lane
Gloucester, Virginia 23061
804 693 3966
877 661 2852
brentandbeckysbulbs.com

Broken Arrow Nursery
13 Broken Arrow Road
Hamden, Connecticut 06518
203 288 1026
brokenarrownursery.com

Buddy's Pool & Spa
10715 York Road
Cockeysville, Maryland 21030
410 666 1800
buddypool.com

W. Atlee Burpee & Co.
300 Park Avenue
Warminster, Pennsylvania 18974
800 888 1447
burpee.com

Companion Plantings
628 Piccadilly Road
Towson, Maryland 21204
410 215 4034

Foxborough Nursery, Inc.
3611 Miller Road
Street, Maryland 21154
410 879 4995
foxboroughnursery.com

Gold Seal Services
6305 Falls Road
Suite 400
Baltimore, Maryland 21209
410 583 1010
dacgllc.com

**Green Fields Nursery
& Landscaping Co.**
5424 Falls Road
Baltimore, Maryland 21210
410 323 3444
greenfieldsnursery.com

C. Grimaldis Gallery
523 N. Charles Street
Baltimore, Maryland 21201
410 539 1080
cgrimaldisgallery.com

Happy Hollow Nurseries
12212 Happy Hollow Road
Cockeysville, Maryland 21030
By appointment only:
410 252 4026

Harris Metalsmith Studio
1760 Principio Furnace Road
Perryville, Maryland 21903
443 553 6642
harrismetalsmith.com

Heartwood Nursery & Garden Shop
8957 Hickory Road
Felton, Pennsylvania 17322
717 993 5230
heartwoodnurseryinc.com

High Country Gardens
223 Avenue D
Suite 30
Williston, Vermont 05495
800 925 9387
highcountrygardens.com

Hugh Lofting Timber Framing, Inc.
339 Lamborntown Road
West Grove, Pennsylvania 19390
610 444 5382
hughloftingtimberframe.com

G. Krug & Son
415 W. Saratoga Street
Baltimore, Maryland 21201
410 752 3166
gkrugandson.com

D. Landreth Seed Co.
582 Highway Route 20
P.O. Box 165
Sharon Springs, New York 13459
800 654 2407
landrethseeds.com

The Lawn Crew
P.O. Box 26163
Baltimore, Maryland 21210
410 882 3356
thelawncrew.net

Lilypons Water Gardens
6800 Lily Pons Road
Adamstown, Maryland 21710
800 999 5459
lilypons.com

Little Greenhouse
9845 Harford Road
Parkville, Maryland 21234
410 661 4748

Maxalea, Inc.
900 Oak Hill Road
Baltimore, Maryland 21239
410 377 7500
maxalea.com

McLean Nurseries
9000 Satyr Hill Road
Parkville, Maryland 21234
410 882 6714

**Meyer Seed Company
of Baltimore, Inc.**
600 S. Caroline Street
Baltimore, Maryland 21231
410 342 4224
meyerseedco.com

Natural Concerns
53 Loveton Circle
Suite 112
Sparks, Maryland 21152
410 472 6860
naturalconcerns.com

NaturaLawn of America
811 Shandy Brook Drive
Westminster, Maryland 21157
410 833 0080
naturalawn.com

The Painted Garden, Inc.
304 Edge Hill Road
Glenside, Pennsylvania 19038
215 884 7378
thepaintedgardeninc.com

**Radebaugh Florist
& Greenhouses**
120 E. Burke Avenue
Towson, Maryland 21286
410 825 4300
radebaugh.com

RareFind Nursery
957 Patterson Road
Jackson, New Jersey 08527
732 833 0613
rarefindnursery.com

Organizations

Saunders Brothers
2717 Tye Brook Highway
Piney River, Virginia 22964
434 277 5455
saundersbrothers.com

Seasons Past Farm and Gardens
825 White Hall Road
Littlestown, Pennsylvania 17340
717 359 0028
seasonspastfarm.com

Stebbins Anderson Co., Inc.
The Shops at Kenilworth
802 Kenilworth Drive
Towson, Maryland 21204
410 823 6600

Swan Island Dahlias
995 N.W. 22nd Avenue
P.O. Box 700
Canby, Oregon 97013
800 410 6540
dahlias.com

Urban Designs
1028 Union Avenue
Baltimore, Maryland 21211
410 952 1832
urbandesignsbmore.com

Valley View Farms
11035 York Road
Cockeysville, Maryland 21030
410 527 0700
valleyviewfarms.com

**Van Engelen Inc. /
John Scheepers, Inc.**
23 Tulip Drive
P.O. Box 638
Bantam, Connecticut 06750
860 567 8734
860 567 0838
vanengelen.com
johnscheepers.com

Viette Nurseries, Inc.
994 Long Meadow Road
Fishersville, Virginia 22939
800 575 5538
viette.com

Watson's Garden Center
1620 York Road
Lutherville, Maryland 21093
410 321 7300
watsonsgarden.com

Wayside Gardens
One Garden Lane
Hodges, South Carolina 29695
800 845 1124
waysidegardens.com

White Flower Farm
167 Litchfield Road
Morris, Connecticut 06763
800 503 9624
whiteflowerfarm.com

American Horticultural Society
7931 E. Boulevard Drive
Alexandria, Virginia 22308
703 768 5700
ahs.org

Cylburn Arboretum Association
4915 Greenspring Avenue
Baltimore, Maryland 21209
410 367 2217
cylburn.org

**The Federated Garden Clubs
of Maryland**
4915 Greenspring Avenue
Baltimore, Maryland 21209
410 396 4842
fgcofmd.org

The Garden Club of America
14 E. 60th Street, Third Floor
New York, New York 10022
212 753 8287
gcamerica.org

The Garden Conservancy
P.O. Box 219
Cold Spring, New York 10516
845 424 6500
gardenconservancy.org

Horticultural Society of Maryland
P.O. Box 4213
Lutherville, Maryland 21093
410 821 5561
mdhorticulture.org

Irvine Nature Center
11201 Garrison Forest Road
Owings Mills, Maryland 21117
443 738 9200
explorenature.org

Ladew Topiary Gardens
3535 Jarrettsville Pike
Monkton, Maryland 21111
410 557 9570
ladewgardens.com

Longwood Gardens
1001 Longwood Road
Kennett Square, Pennsylvania 19348
610 388 1000
longwoodgardens.org

Maryland Native Plant Society
P.O. Box 4877
Silver Spring, Maryland 20914
mdflora.org

Perennial Plant Association
3383 Schirtzinger Road
Hilliard, Ohio 43026
614 771 8431
perennialplant.org

**Howard Peters Rawlings Conservatory
& Botanic Gardens**
3100 Swann Drive
Baltimore, Maryland 21217
410 396 0008
rawlingsconservatory.org

**Smithsonian Archives of
American Gardens**
P.O. 37012
Capital Gallery, Suite 3300
MCR 506
Washington, D.C. 20013-7012
202 633 5840
*gardens.si.edu/
collections-research/aag.html*

The United States National Arboretum
3501 New York Avenue, N.E.
Washington, D.C. 20002
202 245 2726
usna.usda.gov

Winterthur Museum, Garden & Library
5105 Kennett Pike
Wilmington, Delaware 19735
800 448 3883
winterthur.org

A Gardener's Advice
Penney Hubbard

DESIGN

Take advantage of "borrowed scenery." Use a tree in the background, a peephole through the woodland, or a distant valley as a garden vista.

Garden in layers. Create a backdrop with tall plants such as evergreens and hollies. In the middle, plant viburnums, rhododendrons, and azaleas. Finally, place perennials and annuals in the foreground.

Develop specific areas. Within the garden create areas for play, sitting, strolling, storage, etc. This approach is similar to English garden rooms but without walls.

Use terracing to garden on a hillside. Terracing has been used around the world for centuries to prevent erosion and utilize an otherwise unused hillside – and you can do the same.

Plan carefully before adding a water feature. Like a swimming pool, water features are more work than might be imagined.

Choose plants that provide interest all year long. Look for plants with bloom, bark, and fall color interest, or conifers with interesting shapes for winter.

Don't try to create a perfect garden. Nature has a way of spoiling the best-laid plans.

PLANTING

Investigate the soil with a shovel. There is no substitute for digging in the dirt to learn about soil consistency and plant horticulture.

Study the garden to identify its microclimates. Even small gardens contain areas where water puddles, winds blow harshly, and intense sunlight raises the temperature. The highs and lows in a garden affect its various climates.

Improve garden drainage. If plants sit in water, they will have root rot. Frost also flows like water and settles in low spots.

Plant densely. It will result in fewer weeds and less mulch.

Plant certain plants in colonies. Some plants need a lot of company. Three-dozen *Polygonatum odoratum* (Solomon's seal) work well and at least four rows of corn.

Learn about invasive plants. Every experienced gardener has a list, which varies according to climate and taste. Some include: *Houttuynia cordata, Tradescantia virginiana*, and *Lamium maculatum*.

Discover native plants. There are big benefits from plantings accustomed to the area climate. Native plants often do better than plants from other regions.

Try a new plant every year. Something new refreshes the garden and the gardener.

MAINTENANCE

Skip an automatic watering system. They often fail and drown the plants. Instead, for direct delivery and water conservation, use soaker hoses.

Refine the watering schedule. Water in the morning or the afternoon, and not at night, especially in the humid mid-Atlantic. This minimizes disease.

Use a hatchet to divide *Hemerocallis* (daylilies). It's not for the faint of heart.

Leave seedpods on plants. The birds will love them.

Harvest vegetables before first frost. Pick and wrap green tomatoes in newspaper.

Don't worry about failures. View every tree or plant loss as an opportunity.

PESTS

Know when the locusts are coming. They will decimate tender, young tree limbs.

Avoid pesticides. They often harm beneficial insects and the environment.

Learn about companion planting. It attracts helpful insects. Marigolds deter nematodes, and orange rinds turned upside down capture slugs.

Discourage rodents. Spray bulbs with rodent deterrent before planting.

Encourage pollinators. Pollinators and beneficial insects thrive on native plants.

EDUCATION

Start a garden library. Share the books with other gardeners.

Read garden catalogs and garden blogs. "Garden Rant," "Red Dirt Ramblings," and "Everyday Gardener" have strong voices and good information.

Visit gardens. Looking at others' gardens increases knowledge. Gardeners are interesting people who love to swap plants, seeds, ideas, and lessons learned.

Get to know the staff of local nurseries. The most knowledgeable will stand out and become trusted advisors.

Seek out a community of gardeners. Join a garden club or a local chapter of the American Horticultural Society.

Expand garden horizons. Go on garden tours and take courses at a community college, agricultural extension, arboretum, or botanical garden.

Bonsai tools: A kit contains four or five different tools. Great for troughs or tight and tiny spaces.

Broom: It's good for cleanup after a project and enhances all of the work.

Digging shovel: A pointed blade on a 48-inch-long handle. Good for digging, planting, cutting sod, and small roots.

Hand pruners: For a clean cut of stems and small branches. Curved, bypass-style is the easiest to use.

Hand trowel: A short-handled trowel. Used for planting and weeding.

Hoe: Both a long-handled and short-handled version. Good for breaking up soil.

Hori-hori knife: Most come with a sheath that attaches to a belt. For digging, cutting, weeding, dividing.

Ikebana scissors: Flower-arranging-style scissors. Wonderful for the cutting garden.

Lady shovel: A small 30-inch shovel with a D-grip. Easy to manage and fits into tight places.

Loppers: Ratcheting-style shears. More cutting power for branch removal. Easy to use.

Narrow rake: A narrow, eight-inch spring rake. Works between shrubs and perennials.

Transplanting spade: A 46-inch, D-handled, narrow-bladed shovel for digging deep holes and planting.

Tree pruner: Fourteen-foot size with power lever pruner and wood jigsaw combined. Better than using a ladder. Do not stand on ladders to prune.

Watering can: The old-fashioned, galvanized steel version needs to come inside in winter, so ice won't rust out the bottom.

Acknowledgments

On Memorial Day weekend 2013, the telephone rang as I was leaving for an art opening at Cylburn Arboretum in Baltimore. Penney Hubbard was calling to say she wanted to do a book about her garden and asked if I would be the writer.

In 2004, I had written an article about the Hubbards' garden for *Baltimore Style* magazine. Besides Penney's intelligence, humility, and unfailing good disposition during the process of bringing a garden to magazine readers, her attention to plant names was unforgettable.

Two years and five months after her May 2013 phone call, we present the fruits of our collaboration: a book, *On Walnut Hill*: *The Evolution of a Garden*, and a corresponding exhibition at Cylburn Arboretum. I am deeply grateful to Penney and A.C. Hubbard for the most gratifying project of my writing life. I could ask for no finer subject than their garden and family.

I'd like to express my admiration for the team of professionals responsible for assisting us with this book: landscape photographer Roger Foley of Arlington, Virginia; nurseryman Allen Bush of Louisville, Kentucky, who returned to Walnut Hill to write the foreword; Laura Wexler, editor; designer Glenn Dellon; John T. Fitzpatrick, Ph.D., horticulture editor; Chris Zang, copy editor; and Karen C. Smith, exhibition and events coordinator. Working with each has been stimulating and humbling.

The next generation of Hubbards gave new ideas: Hadley Feiss inspired the pages on favorite tools and planting advice; and Crawford Hubbard solved various logistical issues, as did Kimberly Cashman. Publishing advice came from Sarah Achenbach, Ed and Ann Berlin, Darielle Linehan, Bill McAllen, Greg Sesek, Lauren Small, and Margaret Haviland Stansbury. For research, Kay Berney and Joseph M. Coale proved invaluable, as did Martha Marani. The critique of first reader Betty Ann Howard improved this story. Final reader Caroline McKeldin Wayner made sure all was in order.

Electric thanks for the technical savvy of Josh Miller in Wyoming and Greg Pierce, Julie Smith, Jane Daniel, Nigel Assam, and Sam Morgan at Sparks! that launched Walnut Hill into cyberspace; to David Simpson for aerial photography; to Greg Otto for visual review; and to David Orbock and Brian Miller at Full Circle for producing and installing a panoramic exhibition of the book.

Without horticultural expertise, this book would have holes. Perennial thanks to Peter Bieneman, Joel Cohen, Richard Cole, Curry and Roland Harvey, the late Kurt Bluemel, who spoke eloquently about the Hubbards and their garden, and Hannah Bluemel, who continues his legacy.

I'd also like to express my gratitude to Elizabeth Eck of The Tribune Publishing Co., for publishing my first essay 20 years ago. I never planned to be a garden writer, so indelible thanks to Kay MacIntosh, founding editor of *Baltimore Style* magazine, who decided I would be, and to the editors who have followed her. When she was features editor at *The Baltimore Sun*, the late Mary Corey widened my scope, as did Catherine Mallette in her time as *Chesapeake Home* editor. Larry Perl, *The Baltimore Messenger* editor, and Susan G. Dunn, *Baltimore Fishbowl* editor, continue to today.

Never imagining a gardening life, I discovered that genes and surroundings prevail. A strong corps of gardening friends and family members have inspired me, especially my grandparents, Drummond and Katharine Hunt, who discovered the garden I tend today; my parents, Earle and Margaret Hudson, who renovated it, then taught me what to do; and Henry and Elizabeth Otto, who encouraged me. Onward and upward to the youngest: Pete and Merielle Hooker, already bitten by the garden bug.

—Kathy Hudson

Index of Plant Names